"Jim weaves together heartfelt personal stories with tested strategies to increase the FITness of your business, relationships, and personal pursuits. I recommend *Getting FIT* to anyone who wants to shed the excess weight of inefficient teams or a passionless life."

—**John Busacker**, President of INVENTURE – The Purpose Company

"I paid this book the high compliment of giving it to my oldest daughter, who is just beginning her career after recently graduating from college. It reminds us that life without purpose is really no life at all."

—**John Coleman**, CEO and Founder – The VIA Agency

"Jim's FIT strategies apply to my work as an executive recruiter in every way. Bringing the right professionals together is what we do. *Getting FIT* should be required reading material for all recruiters and employers making hiring decisions."

—**Patrick Quinn**, President and Founding Partner—
Quinn Sheridan Executive Search

"Jim Leighton is a high-level leader of leaders whose character, wisdom and intentionality are contagious. FIT accurately provides the missing link in leadership that if applied, will powerfully enhance your life, your leadership and those you're entrusted to lead. That is exactly what it did for me!"

—**Phil Kassel**, Associate Pastor of Family Ministries – Cooksville, Tennessee

"Practical experience-based wisdom for helping teams realize their full potential. A very approachable and worthy read."

—**Douglas R. Conant**, Former President, CEO and Director—Campbell Soup Company, *New York Times* best-selling author of *TouchPoints*

"The path to personal and professional fulfillment could not be clearer. Jim's sage wisdom and experience hands us a map, leading to sustainable success. Looking to improve your life and advance your organization–then focus on *Getting FIT*!"

—**Greg Salciccioli**, Founder and President—Coachwell, Author of *The Enemies of Excellence*

"I found this material immediately actionable. In the week between my first read and my second, I was conscious of employing the principles of FIT."

—**Duane Primozich**, Senior Vice President—Smart Balance Inc.

"Few books really get you to stop and reevaluate your approach to life and business. Jim helped me reconnect with the keys to a fulfilling life and a high-impact career. Trust and a shared, clear mission are as important at home as in the business world. I plan to share this book with my family and my team at work."

—**Steve Hughes**, Chairman and CEO – Smart Balance Inc.

"If you think this book is just about team performance, you're in for a gratifying surprise. Jim is a student of life and brings together many significant lessons about meaning, work, leadership and happiness. He links keen insights to a series of steps for bringing almost any kind of team together for greater purpose, effort, outcome and personal well-being."

—**John Delany**, Founder—Giraffe LLC, Author of *Piloting Strategy*

"Jim provides a fresh, compelling case for getting FIT at all levels—organizations, functions, teams and individuals. The book provides powerful examples of the impact of doing so on organizational success and individual happiness. A must read!"

—**William A. Schiemann**, CEO—Metrus Group, Inc, Author of *The ACE Advantage,* Co-Author of *Bullseye!*

"Having seen, firsthand, Jim apply the principles of FIT, I can personally attest to the powerful impact this had on our business results and on people's lives."

—**Dean Hollis**, Retired President, COO—ConAgra Foods

"Observing Jim and his team apply the principles of FIT at Perdue over the past six years has had, and will continue to have, a significant positive impact on our business. I also appreciate the way it "fits like a glove" with the Perdue values. Simply stated, this stuff works!"

—**Jim Perdue**, Chairman—Perdue Farms Inc.

GETTING

FIT ™

UNLEASH THE POWER OF
FULLY INTEGRATED TEAMS

JIM LEIGHTON

To my father Bill Leighton,

for passing the torch of his leadership

and the integrity of his name on to

a very grateful son.

I cannot celebrate the success of holding this book in my hands without thanking several people whose contributions were crucial to its formation. Everything about *Getting FIT* was a team effort, and I want to recognize the individuals who've shaped this vision into reality.

I extend a special thanks to my design team at Studio Absolute, Russ McIntosh and Cheryl McIntosh, my prolific editor Thomas Womack at BookOx, Eric Weber of Jerico LLC, my typesetter Gary Tompkins, and Lauren Ruef for her research and editorial assistance. Your collective talents and gifts in transforming a raw product into an actionable resource are truly astonishing.

I pause to thank my father, Bill Leighton, and a host of other mentors including my life coach Greg Salciccioli who was strategic and relentless to ensure this book moved from a dream to a reality. I thank my wife, Fritzi, for her constant support, my daughter, Lauren, for her teacher's insight, and my son, Jimmy, for his enthusiasm and contributions to this work: you are my home team. To my mother, Phyllis, I owe tremendous gratitude and love for nurturing my curiosity as a child and training me as a man and a leader.

My brother Bill's candid story of rediscovering his FIT profoundly enriched this work. I thank him for demonstrating an unwavering commitment to serve people with his surgical skills and passions. I also extend thanks to my friend Phil Kassel for sharing his story, to my sister, Anne, for her special insight, and to countless others whose expertise and suggestions brought depth and dimension to this resource.

A special thanks to Jim Perdue for his genuine leadership and generosity in helping FIT to come alive at Perdue. A big thanks also to the talented individuals I've labored alongside at various companies, whose lives have filled the pages of this book with authenticity and humor. I'm grateful too for my lifelong mentors and friends who've endorsed this book and become advocates of FIT.

Finally, to my reader: thank you for the opportunity to speak into your life. This work is from my heart, and I trust it will ignite a dynamic and active change in yours. It's been a tremendous experience to share the stage with so many gifted people in my fifty-six years of life. I stand in the backlight of each success, celebrating it as a mutual victory and thanking my Heavenly Father for the gift of people and their passions.

Contents

Foreword

We spend a lot of time and energy obsessing over how we can become better as individuals. This is good. Personal excellence is a critical component to a fulfilling life. But you can only get so far on your own. There comes a time when leaders must empower others to become the-best-version-of-themselves, especially those who are on their team at work. Unfortunately, for most people this moment comes far too late in their careers. Perhaps now is the moment for you to think about creating a Fully Integrated Team (FIT).

Too many business books are published with ridiculous and sterile language that does not resonate with real people. FIT is honest in a way that is disarming and refreshing—it is immensely practical.

As you read it, I challenge you to ask yourself three questions at the end of each chapter.

1. How FIT am I?

2. How FIT is my team?

3. What am I going to do about it this week?

The integration Jim discusses in this book will do two incredible things in your life and for your team: the multiplication of talent and energy.

Everyone wants to have their talent multiplied. When we work with others, 1

+ 1 should equal at least 2, but hopefully more than 2. We have all worked with people who have diminished our talent, so that 1 + 1 equaled less than 2. This is incredibly frustrating and exhausting, and often robs us of the fulfillment we should experience at work. This is why everyone loves working with people who have a can-do attitude—those who multiply our efforts.

Just as we want to have our talent multiplied, we yearn to experience fulfillment at work and crave the enthusiasm that is born through it. How many people do you know who are truly enthusiastic about their work? Great leaders energize people by integrating teams in ways that respect individuals and unleash the power in numbers.

It sounds great, but few of us are ever taught how to do it. Get ready, as you are about to learn.

FIT has some of the best insights I have ever read about finding meaning in our work and bringing meaning to our work.

Matthew Kelly, President—Floyd Consulting, *New York Times* best-selling author of *The Dream Manager*

Introduction
Something Bigger and More Meaningful

In my thirty-five years in the consumer packaged goods industry, I've had the privilege of applying FIT to well over 100,000 people. I've founded, run, sold, and even allowed for the bankruptcy of my own start-up, and met with more successes as well as failures than most people have.

Meanwhile, along that lengthy path, two primary questions surfaced unanswered, year after year:

First, why do some people, organizations, married couples, and societies find fulfillment—while others do not?

And second, why are some of these individuals and groups able to sustain a higher level of success for a longer period of time than others?

People and organizations have different ways of measuring success, but a common definition lies in finding a sense of meaning and purpose at work.

At the intersection of organizational success and individual success is a concept I call FIT. Essentially, that's an acronym for Fully Integrated Teams. That's the core meaning behind the many occurrences of "FIT" you'll see in this book. It is, however, a very wide-ranging concept built around a tight cluster of principles and core values with practical application on a number of fronts. So at certain points here—especially as it concerns your own progress and direction in life and career—you can even expand the meaning of FIT to represent something like "Fully Integrated Trajectory." In light of the steady effectiveness this concept brings to your work and other pursuits, you could also call it "Fully Integrated Traction." And for describing the overall result it brings in an individual's life or in a company or any other organization, you might well think of it as "Fully Integrated and Thriving."

Integration is the key—bringing the right things and the right people together into a dynamic, life-giving combination. It's groups of people who together can create something bigger and more meaningful than any single individual ever could. This brings fulfillment to individuals that touches all the dimensions of spiritual, emotional, intellectual and physical health. And, especially for organizations, this includes the added dimension of being fiscally FIT.

In the pages to come I'll have a lot more to say and show you about all this. I'll pass these things along while I also disclose some defining moments in my own story.

FIT is a big and multifaceted concept. Within this book's limits, I won't be able to give an exhaustive analysis of every aspect of it, because there's so much more that could be expressed and developed. But I will freely share with you highlights of my own experiences that have taught me the most.

I wrote this book on the shoulders of great leaders. One of them is my father, who's had a greater impact on my leadership style and effectiveness than anyone else.

Creating the FIT model has also meant a three-decade process of working with, managing, and learning alongside other people. I've absorbed hundreds of books and expert research on organizational behavior, leadership, and psychology. Authors like Jim Collins, Seth Godin, Matthew Kelly, and my life coach Greg Salciccioli have particularly informed my framework through their insight and experience. They get FIT.

FIT was born out of my curiosity to understand how people find their place in life—good or bad, intentional or careless. I'll touch on some stories of those who've found FIT, those who've lost FIT, as well as those who are still looking for it.

Throughout this book, I'll address both individuals and organizations. Essentially the two are interchangeable, since individuals always need each other, while organizations always need the right people. This sharing of meaningful labor fuels Fully Integrated Teams. It's people with like-minded passions who work toward a cooperative goal and reach the highest levels of achievement as barriers are removed. A Fully

Integrated Team could be a married couple, an athletic team, a family, or a committee of professionals.

Jim Collins says that greatness isn't just a business quest; it's a human quest. I love that statement. *Business* can be a dried-up kind of term that makes us think of systems and processes and buildings instead of people. FIT is about stripping all that away to reveal the most important factor: finding a sense of purpose, and linking with others who are passionate to fulfill it.

Your FIT will define you. At the end of your life, you'll be remembered most by the relationships you developed. There's already a critical mass of people at work in your life. Discover how you can achieve your collective potential with these FIT teams of individuals to accomplish almost anything.

I believe my attempt to expand your mind on these things will bring successful life-change for you. I've seen this happen with others, again and again.

With working adult students at Keller Graduate School of Management in Chicago, my FIT model was put to the test. As an instructor for leadership and organizational behavior classes, I had taught FIT for five consecutive terms when I noticed a trend among my working adult students. After being introduced to FIT, on average two to three students in each class of twenty-five had a significant change in their personal or professional situation. Change was imminent for those students who rigorously applied FIT. Many of them quit their jobs to find a better one elsewhere, some got promoted, and others were reassigned at their request. It also meant new commitments and realizations in their family and friendships.

So let's get started! And if at any time in your FIT journey you have a desire to engage me in conversation or training, please contact me at JimLeighton.com.

Now...let's get FIT!

Part One

**The Power
of Purpose**

Chapter One
Instructive Legacy: My Father's Story

My father's death came in the cold of February. Home for me at the time was in Omaha, but my heart was still stranded at his bedside in Arizona. I watched his strength fray like a thread. The cancer took over. Yet his voice, both strong and clear, still imparts to me this sense of duty: "Of all the things I've given you, my name is the most valuable and important. Treat it with care and dignity, and behave in a way that will make us proud of that name. I gave my name to you untarnished, and I wish for you to do the same for your children, Lauren and Jimmy. I love you."

A plaque that reads "Leighton" is my solid reminder of him. I look at it above my desk at home, and I find it a welcome distraction. Nothing is more important than remembering my beginning, my father's story—the story that compels me to lead others.

Bill Leighton

William "Bill" Leighton was a pilot and gunnery instructor in the U.S. Navy and loved to fly small aircraft, to hunt, and to fish. After serving his country during World War II, he took a job selling baked goods ingredients such as chocolate and vanillin to local commercial bakeries. One of his customers was Mr. Swanson, owner of the Swanson Cookie Company which later became Archway Cookies. My father came to work for Mr. Swanson and later flew his airplane across the country to meet with prospective owners of commercial cookie companies, convincing them to become franchisees of Archway. He was successful in doing so.

When I was three years old, my father became the general manager of Archway's franchise in Riverside, California, after his good friend George Markham assumed ownership of Archway. By the time I was six, we relocated to Ottawa, Illinois, where my father gained ownership in another Archway franchise, Oak State Products. He became the president of his industry's trade association, the Biscuit and Cracker Manufactures Association, while on the local scene he became an active community member as chairman of the board at Ottawa Hospital.

Years later, at my father's funeral, his friend George Markham would approach me and describe my father as "one of those rare people that engaged in meaningful conversations with just about anyone. He had a passion for people and lived his life in the service of others." I couldn't agree more. My dad experienced a true integration with others, and gave himself to help others achieve some experience of this integration themselves.

Life on Catfish Lake

Dad and our dog Piper loving life on the lake

When I was eight, my parents bought a small cabin on Catfish Lake in Wisconsin. The year was 1964. I spent many childhood summers learning to water-ski on just about anything—Ping-Pong paddles, tennis shoes, other people, and even my bare feet. Catfish Lake is where my love of fishing, hunting, and the outdoors was born. We had no television there and certainly no smart phone technology to occupy our time—nothing but an old rotary dialed phone with a phone number beginning with the letters HE.

In these formative years, my parents' support and trust was crucial as the richness of family relationships sustained us. On the basis of that respect and trust, we were a Fully Integrated Team decades before the concept of FIT came together in my mind. I was experiencing it and learning it long before I identified it.

Bill, Phyllis, and me at the lake

The cabin remained a fixture in our family after my father retired. Around the Fourth of July each summer, I would return to Catfish Lake, joined by my wife Fritzi, daughter Lauren, and son Jimmy, and we would celebrate my father's birthday together. We rarely missed his birthday, even as we moved often to different parts of the country.

At the age of seventy-six, "Wild Bill" (as his friends called him) learned how to fly gliders—drift airplanes with no engines that are towed into the sky by another plane. He earned his glider's license after a series of lessons at a small airfield in Three Lakes, Wisconsin. Age was never a deterrent to him; he was always engaged in some kind of hobby.

A Shared Passion

One summer at the lake, my father and I were sitting on the dock enjoying a sunset when he looked up from his Rum and Coke and asked, "Would you like to go do something special in the morning?" I wondered what he meant by *special*. "I can't tell you until we do it," he said. "How about we leave around six-thirty? I want to show you something. But don't tell your mother."

In the secrecy of morning, we slipped out of the cabin and headed for Three

Lakes. We arrived at the local air strip to find a couple of small hangars and a building next to a single runway. I heard a plane coming in for a landing, one of those single-engine crop dusters. I watched it as the owner of Barry Aviation came out to greet us. He was an old friend of my father's.

After the introductions, this spur-of-the-moment trip was beginning to look well-rehearsed. I was licensed to fly single-engine fixed-wing aircraft, but I'd never done aerobatics in a glider before. An easy smile spread across my father's face at his plan's unfolding. The flight instructor ensured me the ride of my life with an audience of one—my father, watching from the airfield below. We'd shared many flights before as father and son. My dad loved to fly and was fortunate to have access to a company aircraft he piloted for much of his career. His inspiration gave my brother, Bill, and me the spirit to fly too.

Getting ready to soar

The instructor handed me something that looked like a seat cushion with two sewn-in straps. It was a parachute, and it spooked me more than I let on. I'd known the sweat-drenched thrill of flight, especially on my first solo to receive my pilot's license years earlier. The memories were flooding back. Afterward,

I even had my shirt tacked up on the wall alongside many other wet-backed newcomers to the pilot's club.

There were only a few instruments in the glider's cockpit, far fewer than in a powered aircraft. It was designed to go fast and stay aloft at the expense of some extra leg room. A stick divided the space between my knees, and my feet hit the pedals. The instructor directly behind me had a second set of controls. I was instructed to put my feet on the pedals and one hand on the stick to understand the basics of takeoff.

With the clear acrylic canopy shut over our heads, we were taxied into position by the tow plane. The tow rope became taut, and the instructor moved the rudder to indicate our readiness for takeoff. As we gained speed down the runway, our wings came level with the ground, and we were quickly aloft in the beautiful blue sky of the northern Wisconsin woods.

The instructor showed me how to box around the propeller wash and the wake of the plane. I couldn't see the turbulence ahead, but I sure could feel it. At ten thousand feet, the tow plane dipped and raised his wings to indicate we were in a good position for release. We returned the message and banked right as the tow plane banked left, and I pulled a lever that released the tow rope between us. With the hum of the plane dying off into the distance, I sensed the beauty of flight. It was so still it felt as if we weren't moving at all. I could see the beautiful blue lakes and green trees below and a few cumulus clouds building in the early sun. It was beautiful, peaceful, and brief.

After obtaining clear and level flight, the instructor let me at the controls. I was now the pilot, monitoring our airspeed with vigilance. At the end of a quick lesson, the instructor asked if I was ready for some aerobatics, per my father's request. He assured me it would be quick, and we would lose a lot of altitude in the process. I agreed, bracing before the unknown.

He assumed full control of the aircraft again and pressed the stick forward, pointing the nose of the glider toward the earth. With the ground in clear view, I grew anxious for what came next. My instructor pulled back on the stick and swung the plane into two quick loops. Coming out of the second loop, he asked me if I was okay. I said yes before the plane reeled again—then deeply regretted it.

With the plane in a perfectly vertical position, we stopped moving upward and let gravity slide us back toward earth again. The feeling was alien and petrifying. The nose of the aircraft went over my head and we tumbled again. By now I was sweating profusely, disoriented from the spinning and spiraling. We'd lost a lot of altitude and were headed in for a landing.

The flight had lasted a mere twenty minutes. On the ground, after the plane's left wing dropped to rest, my instructor popped the canopy open for me to stumble out, my limbs still in a stupor from the flight. My father received us with delight, grinning ear to ear as I struggled in his direction.

"How was it?" He beamed.

"Unbelievable," I said truthfully. "That was so much fun!"

My wife and my mother stood in the kitchen that afternoon as we slinked through the door like two suspects. Green and sweaty, I bypassed their questioning looks, knowing my father would handle the explanation. I went straight to bed and wasn't myself until the next day—a fair trade-off for an unforgettable morning.

This was one of many learning experiences my father gave me, rekindling my passion for flight and setting me on a path to develop the necessary skills to succeed as a pilot. (A few years later, while living in Boulder, Colorado, I took lessons and learned how to fly gliders.) To commemorate that adventurous day, I have a coffee mug bearing a picture of two grown men with giddy smiles. That day with my father is something I'm reminded of by a line in Don McLean's

"American Pie" song: "the three men I admire the most, the Father, Son and the Holy Ghost." If there were a fourth, Bill Leighton would be it.

The Later Years

A more sobering lesson for me arises from my memories of my father's later years.

There was a side of my father that began to decline shortly after our glider experience. If you ask me, before cancer officially took his life, he died of isolation and a lost passion for life. After turning seventy-eight, his interactions with friends and family changed. His new environment was different. His former life had been filled with friends, coworkers, and activities to keep him busy. But a move to Arizona didn't suit him well. Though he was located closer to my brother, Bill, and his family, he was further from the work he knew and loved.

In his prime, my father had been an energetic man, always rapt in the beauty of ordinary life. My sister, Anne, recalls how "he listened attentively to the details of the latest Dr. Seuss book I'd read or how many dandelions I'd skillfully removed from the yard; then he'd pick me up and we danced to the rhythm of the songs he'd taught me. It always amazed me that the entire time I lived at home he had that sparkle in his eyes, genuinely interested in hearing about my day."

He was also humble, seeking to quietly serve others as a coworker and friend. After my father's passing, I learned that he established a scholarship program to sponsor gifted high school musicians. He was somewhat musical himself; he loved to sing on road trips, as Anne recalls: "He created an atmosphere of adventure as we sang the playful lyrics of catchy tunes heading toward our destination. The harmony created a strong sense of alignment and teamwork." Anne remembers me singing along with him as well, and grinning with a sparkle in my eyes matched only by our father's.

For many people who grow older and lose friends, isolation sets in. That was true for my father; a man who was once a charismatic father, friend, and husband became an isolated, paranoid man suffering from deep depression. This saddened his family, and was difficult for us to understand. For my mother, it was almost unbearable.

Watching this process unfold in my father's life was a significant lesson in my own. People need each other, but more than this, they need a compelling reason to live. They need to live a FIT life.

Possibly the most competent individual ever to address this subject was Viktor Frankl, a Holocaust survivor. In his book *Man's Search for Meaning,* Frankl writes,

> *There is nothing in the world, I venture to say, that would so effectively help one to survive even the worst conditions as the knowledge that there is a meaning in one's life.*

He goes on to quote a saying of Nietzsche that he considers central to this wisdom: "He who has a *why* to live can bear with almost any *how.*"

In my own thirty-five years of leadership, I've learned to ask *the* fundamental question of companies, of my coworkers, and of myself. That question is this: *What's the purpose?*

I watched my father succumb to this question with inaudible despair in his later years, despite his loving family and productive career. It's a profound question for each individual; it defines our meaning.

Chapter Two
Connecting the Dots: My Story

Decades ago I flew down to Houston to explore a possible job opportunity. I was still wet behind the ears, with a degree in business and labor relations fresh in hand. At the airport arrivals platform, a white pickup truck approached with a gun rack in the back window. I was expecting the HR manager from a large oil refinery, but not like this.

With a furtive glance to ensure no gun was in the rack, I hopped in.

On our drive to the hotel, the man had difficulty holding conversation because his jaw was wired shut. He dropped me off, then came by later to take me to a Houston Oilers game. Over a couple of beers, I mustered up enough courage to ask what happened to his jaw. Instead he told me what happened to the "other guy"—who looked far worse, he assured me, after their scuffle in a local bar.

The next morning we toured the oil refinery where I tried not to notice the intolerable humidity. The main office, housing the plant manager and his staff, was a security fortress. That was my first hint at the elephant in the room. Mediating between management, the union, and the hourly associates was a job that meant walking a tightrope of already tense relationships. The air of superiority I sensed behind the secure walls of this nice office wasn't helping. The union and the hourly associates would surely frame me as their newfound enemy. To put it mildly, there would be no hero's welcome for me.

A job offer came on the heels of that visit which I ultimately declined, going with my gut reaction. I sensed the disintegrated teamwork at the oil company and knew my efforts would be futile in that perfect storm of animosity. Upon my return to Illinois, I sold life insurance to buy some time. I had to think about how to jump-start my career. The college training wheels were off, and life came careening at me full force.

The Picture We Paint

We all have this experience of connecting the dots to form an intelligible pattern in our lives. We call this pattern a *career,* and it begins with simply drawing the lines from A to B: high school to college, college to graduate school, and graduate school to full-time work. But there, we pause. Asked now to plot the course ourselves, we fear creating our own possibilities.

For this reason, some of us do the easier wrong thing instead of the harder right thing. Some find a job, almost any job, where another person will place the dots for them. Driven by fear, these individuals would rather "paint by the numbers" than use their own artistry, imagination, and resolve to plot the course. They're the victims of circumstance.

Maybe that was you. At times, it was me.

Going forward, you'll connect your own dots. So open your mind as you continue reading, pick up your paintbrush, and fill your palette with rich and vibrant colors to plot an illustration of your desired future state. Be a victor over your own life. Take control, and discover how the tenacity for both great risk and dreams will land you right where you need to be. To do this requires the right FIT.

Finding our Fully Integrated Team provides a framework through which to view ourselves, our past, our current situation, and our future. It teaches us how to become the artist of our lives.

And it begins with understanding the power of *purpose.*

Recovering a Sense of Purpose

What happens to a company when its people lack an understanding of their purpose or importance? That's something I learned when I arrived at ConAgra's plant in Batesville, Arkansas.

Morale there was low and turnover high, with hourly associates dropping like flies. Work-related accidents occurred at an alarming rate, and product quality control was a major problem. In my first meeting with the plant manager, I anticipated a man exasperated about the plant's declining condition. Instead, he disclosed a shrewd business technique that accounted for the whole unhappy lot of his employees. He began by saying, "I'm saving the company money"— which seemed fair enough, until he explained how. The associates were paid an hourly rate that increased over the first year of their probationary period with ConAgra. He explained that if he could keep his hourly associates from making it through their first year, he wouldn't have to pay them the higher rate they earned.

The Purpose Model

Hearing this, I didn't know whether to cry or laugh; on the inside I was doing both. This plant manager meant to perpetuate his own turnover problem, as if it were a fiscally responsible new management technique. I assured him it wasn't. He didn't yet understand the power of a Fully Integrated Team. No one at his plant had a vested interest in the company, in the work process, or in the product of their work. No one cared—and it bore a heavy cost on his employees and stakeholders.

Those of us closest to it know the problem best: *people in the American workplace have lost their sense of purpose.* We've been on teams or committees lacking much of anything to be proud of. Maybe we're holding the reins of leadership in the least desirable moment; we feel we're at the helm of a sinking ship. We might be trudging through the motions at work because there's no real connection between who we are and what we do. In the midst of everything, we've lost our *purpose*, our reason for being.

Personally, it might begin with questions like these: *Why should I be passionate about fulfilling this role? Why do I get out of bed in the morning, aside from an obligation or a paycheck? Do I really know what my skills are, and am I working to master them? Who am I really helping?*

Leaders are consumed with the *people* in their organizations; they understand that people make the difference between a powerhouse team and a wilting, dysfunctional committee. It's all about "getting the right people on the bus," as Jim Collins has emphasized. But if each member, or the team itself, lacks a clear understanding of *purpose*, it's impossible to have unity.

Purpose is simply understanding one's reason for being driven by personal values and deep-seated beliefs. A *purpose* is the foundation of any team working toward a collective goal.

People, Products, Profitability

The Batesville plant was experiencing a lack of purpose—and it wasn't my first tangle with this kind of problem in the consumer packaged goods industry. So I spent the next few months developing an organizational purpose statement for

ConAgra—a reason for being, and how this supported the corporate vision. The plant manager and I established acceptable and unacceptable cultural norms. We published a set of shared principles that the Batesville employees felt passionate about. Then we established people goals for reducing turnover, improving safety, and intensifying the engagement of hourly associates at work.

Jim enjoying a conversation with a frontline associate

On target to becoming an organization that cared, we turned our focus next to *product goals*, starting with quality. We wanted the associates to be proud of the products they made. We posted work aids and pictures of acceptable and unacceptable products along the production lines. We put a visual performance board in common areas around the plant to track key performance indicators and to demonstrate what was working. We placed the people goals and charts on the left side of the board, the product goals in the middle, and the productivity measures on the far right, indicating how the company aligned its commitments: first people, then products, before profits.

The culture of this plant shifted from its singular focus on budgets and productivity to an atmosphere *where people found meaning in their work*. We created Fully Integrated Teams around various processes in the plant, and we explained to people why we were taking a different approach.

A year after being implemented, this process was institutionalized. The performance of the Batesville plant went on to demonstrate its success. We created value for all stakeholders, especially our newfound leaders and their followers.

Turnover dropped by over 80 percent, product quality and customer service were enhanced, and productivity shot through the roof. The company cared for its people, and the people cared for the company. We created high-energy teams, and the hourly associates were actually enjoying their work again. They no longer labored for a paycheck but for the sake of a team that enjoyed being together. They took so much pride in what they produced that some employees even began proselytizing customers in the grocery store, explaining how ConAgra products are made. Their attitude shifted from one of *obligation* to one of *ownership*.

FIT Working Relationships

With Dean Hollis, my friend and former supervisor at ConAgra, I now share a position on the board of directors of Smart Balance, Inc. Dean was president at ConAgra when I was senior vice president over multiple plants, including Batesville. Batesville was just one of many success stories we shared while working as a FIT team. Speaking of FIT, Dean once told me, "What we did at ConAgra was remarkable, but *how* you did it was magical. Once people see and feel what you're doing, they become interested and want to be a part of it."

In my days with Dean at ConAgra, there was a time when things got a little off-track in my area of responsibility and needed tightening up. Dean sent me a three-word email memo to bring it to my attention: "Wobble, wobble,

wobble." He trusted me to fix what was loose, and that's all it took. Dean and I had a wonderful working relationship.

At the Batesville plant, FIT began with a desired future state of high morale and less turnover, and it was achieved in gaining maximum engagement from the hourly associates. In creating a FIT team, the desired future state was realized and celebrated with fulfilled employees and a better product offering, or what I refer to as an organization's *promise*—the uniquely relevant value or service that it provides to others (we'll look closer at this later).

Many have denied that a high level of engagement and motivation is possible within the kind of employment scenario I've just described. Employee potential is bypassed when companies refuse to see how their culture shapes work ethic. Hourly wage positions like coffee baristas or factory workers are often considered only temporary or menial forms of work inconsequential to cultivating meaning in the employee's life. In my experience, this is a falsehood.

The root cause of disengagement can often be traced to a lack of good leadership. Leaders are more than figureheads and bosses. They're team players who know their own strengths and can pinpoint those of their followers. They spur organizations and teams toward effective change, making the workplace a dynamic and active place where individual strengths are rewarded. As Seth Godin reminds us, there's a difference between someone who leads and someone who manages: "Leaders have followers. Managers have employees." Followers join the cause even when they don't have to, and they trust even when they could withhold that trust. But employees just do what they're told.

Working as a salaried manager alongside hourly associates has taught me more about my leadership and responsibility to a team than any other experience. I've led thousands of people in my senior management roles at Nabisco, Celestial Seasonings, the Hain-Celestial Group, ConAgra Foods, and Perdue Farms Inc., with direct responsibility for multibillion-dollar businesses and over one hundred thousand people at eighty manufacturing plants. None of this has come at the expense of realizing my own mistakes and building on my strengths. I serve on many boards of directors; I'm a mentor to many people, and I receive professional coaching to maintain transparency in my life and leadership. As a whole, the decisions I've made in my career are ones I'm proud of. My desire is now to share my success with others through passing along to them the FIT process.

Bus Driver or Ditch Digger?

It wasn't always this way. A future in leadership was the last thing on my mind as a high school kid in a small town in Illinois. I'd graduated in the bottom half of my class, and I found athletics much more interesting than academics. I had little if any awareness of my purpose, and I hadn't developed solid principles for how to live my life. At the top of my game as captain of the swim and golf teams, I was tunnel-visioned, rarely wondering what more I could become.

Concerned with my poor academic performance, my parents hauled me up to the Illinois Institute of Technology in Chicago, a ninety-minute drive from our home, for a psychological and intellectual testing analysis. If the name of that test didn't put the fear of God in me, the outcome would. The recommendation from this prestigious institute and from the Ph.D. who administered my tests was that I was best suited to drive a bus or dig ditches. That proclamation, to my shame, was shared with both my parents.

I assessed my options: I could do something to change—or accept digging ditches or driving a bus as my future. I knew I hadn't mustered up the grades for anyone to expect better of me, but deep down I knew there was more to me than this test had identified. So I swallowed my pride and decided I was going to change.

Irving Berlin said that life is 10 percent what you make it and 90 percent how you take it. To challenge that ditch-digger prediction of my future, I went on to earn a business degree in labor relations with a minor in psychology and an MBA and became a senior faculty member teaching MBA students. Since then, no one has ever placed a limit on what I'm capable of—such limits can come only from *me*. Through my own thoughts, beliefs, and actions, I've demonstrated that success is attainable in my life. *I* was the only person I held responsible for making that change happen.

A Dream Team

Over the years I've developed an uncompromising penchant for doing the right thing for the right reason. Early in my career, I owned my own business and was too focused on the extrinsic trappings of my life before my purpose and principles. As I gained more emotional intelligence through experience and study, a FIT foundation is now in place from which I operate and make decisions. This, joined with patience and hard work, has helped me find my passion. It has led me to memorable partnerships where my needs, skills, and passions are aligned to serve people in a nutrient-rich environment.

I found myself in several leadership roles with Nabisco. One memorable FIT moment came early in my career, shortly before taking the reins at the company's Niles plant. In my seven years with Nabisco, I cut my teeth in consumer packaged goods within the food and beverage space. Nabisco remains a great company to this day, filled with great people and brands.

Ellen Marram, then president of Nabisco, hired me as the senior manager of specialty contracting. Nabisco sought to grow beyond its share of the cookie and cracker aisle in retail grocery stores, and Ellen had a great idea. Nabisco's commanding market share needed to create future growth. We decided to look at ourselves differently—as a snack food company. We expressed this in our new mission statement that read: "Goodness in snacking, any time, anywhere." The "anywhere" is where my role came in. The vision was to gain a greater share of our consumer's stomach through innovative and relevant snack food products.

Ellen created a FIT by aligning top executives within Nabisco. I was the only member on the team of six who was new to the company. Ellen pulled us together and charted our course. She told us that she was our internal sponsor, and that our objective was to leverage and utilize all of Nabisco's great brands, talent, and know-how to create new products to merchandise outside the cookie and cracker aisle.

We were free to use whichever brands we had and to create new ones, and were directed to get new products to market expediently, without manufacturing the products internally. Leveraging the contract manufacturers to produce our finished product was my role. The FIT was highly energized and delivered against our charter. The new products launched faster than any internally manufactured product. The line we created included Oreo and Teddy Graham Ice Cream Cones, as well as Oreo, Nilla, and Nutter Butter Pie Shells, in addition to an entire line of granola bars released under a variety of existing brands.

This was a team of mavericks—what Warren Bennis refers to as a "Great Group." We were separated from the mother ship but fueled with the resources we needed. I loved what I was doing. Utilizing my father's ties to the cookie and cracker industry, I networked extensively to finish the project.

We released our new product launch less than one year from its conception. Soon after, Ellen left the company for an opportunity to lead Seagram's and Tropicana. Without her sponsorship and effort to keep the internal wolves and internal red tape at bay, our Fully Integrated Team was brought to its knees by internal politics and forced to do things the Nabisco way.

An Improvement Mind-Set

There will always be some kind of opposition to Fully Integrated Teams seeking to do great things. Those driven by negative thinking are unhappy with their own success and unfortunately diminish opportunities for others to have it. This is why at Perdue we focus on healthy team dynamics guided by the following "Improvement Mind-Set" principles that optimize success:

- I make decisions based on facts.
- I see problems as hurdles to overcome, not as barriers.
- I challenge experts' conclusions and constraints.
- I take responsibility for making people and projects succeed.
- I celebrate the small victories, and I encourage others.
- I help set clear priorities based on facts.
- I work to fully and completely understand the other person.
- I seek to understand before being understood.
- My actions and behaviors demonstrate that I'm committed to and aligned with the company's values, vision, aspirations, and reason for being.

Our team's collapse at Nabisco didn't sour my taste for the company, but signaled a new opportunity with the Niles plant. There I received greater responsibilities and learning experiences which eventually landed me at Perdue—where I've had the rare privilege of shaping a company's people, culture, and future. I've never taken that responsibility lightly. When I get up in the morning, things are rarely perfect at my job or otherwise. There are dysfunctions and maladies to address, both in systems and in people. But each morning, there are people I love to see and things I get to do, and I'm grateful for it.

The choice to lead others rewards me well beyond a paycheck. The journey is certainly not problem-free, but has led me to a place of deep contentment in my work. My cultivation of FIT is an important process that's molded and shaped me into a better leader and listener. I haven't always "got it right," but in those moments of questioning myself—moments where I misjudged my company's culture or an individual's skill set—I've learned something valuable: most people will rise to the occasion if they're supported.

We all want to be a part of the greater whole, to make something big of our lives and to make it count as a legacy. In working toward a FIT life, we're doing just that.

Chapter Three
Lost and Found: My Brother's Story

Soon after we lived through the journey of my father's last days on earth, a lack of purpose haunted my brother's life. Despite a lucrative medical career, a question was gnawing at Bill: "Why should I get up and go to work today, aside from my paycheck? What's the use in all this?"

A Moment of Fear

The voice at the other end of the phone gave a measured response: "It's Judy." As she continued, the fear in my sister-in-law's words was an avalanche at bay, looming over our conversation. She meant for me to come to Arizona.

"What's wrong?" I asked.

Strong for the moment, she was impatient with my need for further details. She needed my presence. Everything else would be explained upon my arrival.

Family means more to me than that list of contacts on an "in case of emergency" form. And so I went.

Dr. William Leighton living FIT 2012

Thoughts of my brother commenced on the flight over. A reconstructive plastic surgeon, he had exhausted himself to acquire an M.D. for the end of our family name. I respected him immensely for it. Judy earned something close to sainthood in tending to the needs of their two sons while my brother became a renowned surgeon and medical professional. The boys were in law school now, Josh at Arizona State and Jason at Pepperdine.

I remembered visiting Bill in medical school at the University of Illinois when his passion for the medical field was unshakable. He took me to the cadaver lab there, where his colleague worked out of a black body bag while eating a hamburger at the same time. I never forgot that strange sight.

The turbulence on the flight to Phoenix rattled loose some emerging concerns. Two weeks prior to my arrival in Arizona, Bill had been scheduled for surgery just like any other day. But on that day, Dr. Leighton was a no-show. Patients came to his waiting room and weren't seen. His reputation at work was otherwise flawless; he never missed a day. Now, without warning or explanation, he became a recluse, virtually disappearing from his family life and workplace.

The Doctor Is Out

Bill rarely left his bedroom for reasons beyond food. The first time I saw him, bedraggled and garbed in a white robe, he emerged from his self-imposed prison. He was only a semblance of the brother I'd known, and it unnerved me. Naturally, a question like "What can I do to help?" wouldn't be received well. But I asked anyway. The despondence in his eyes and a terse "nothing" answered me enough, before my mind wandered over the events of recent months.

My father's death was still a fresh wound for us all. Medically speaking, Bill knew exactly what was happening from the little white cancer spots on the X-ray, yet the emotional element he kept at bay. In my last visit to see my father at the hospital, Bill and my mother were there. The attending doctor explained that my father was not in pain, but if left on life support, his lungs would fill up with liquid, resulting in a struggle for breath.

Bill understood this reality. But his feelings were frozen, kept in check by virtue of his professional medical training. Stuffed and ignored, maybe his unresolved grief was finally surfacing. With the heart-wrenching but settled decision to remove my father's life support, Bill remained at his side—the son his father was so very proud of, and the son who, though a highly skilled physician, could not save his father's life. I wondered if Bill still struggled with that helplessness.

Bill's involvement in a malpractice lawsuit prefaced my father's death. With the threat of legal action overshadowing even the best of surgeons in Bill's line of work, he now faced a patient who claimed in court that she was harmed by a botched surgery performed by one of his colleagues. Bill was asked to testify as an expert witness for the plaintiff in the case. The patient won and the doctor lost, resulting in a complaint against my brother for false and deceptive testimony. Bill was eventually exonerated, yet, the accusations took a toll. Was this bearing heavily on his mind?

Changing Course

Plastic surgeons flocked to the better pay differential offered in elective cosmetic procedures. Even skilled heart surgeons, Bill knew, were completing plastic surgery residencies to make a better living. It was difficult for the best surgeons to charge sufficient rates for their services with the decrease in usual and customary rates paid to physicians by insurance companies. So the surgeons in highest demand altered their practices to cash-on-the-barrel elective aesthetic procedures like face-lifts, tummy-tucks, and breast implants. My brother jumped on the cash bandwagon when he had the chance, causing a paradigm shift in his motivation for practicing medicine. He began to lose his *purpose,* as the lure of money replaced his passion. That's when the trouble began.

With an abrupt greeting and a few minutes of strained interaction between us, Bill retreated behind a closed door in his Paradise Valley home. Judy studied my reaction, familiar with her own failed attempts to communicate with her husband. I now understood why I'd come. Even as Bill's crisis appeared unexpectedly, like rain from a cloudless sky, somewhere there loomed a thunderhead at fault. I was running headlong toward all the warning signs that would lead me to the source of his despair.

Bill prefaced slide show presentations to colleagues with pictures of his palatial mansion, showcasing his lucrative earnings in plastics. Here my brother demonstrated the "hubris of success." Arrogant, he lost sight of his *purpose,* the guiding motivation behind his work: to help people regain a normal life.

The "undisciplined pursuit of more" had brought Bill to this place, where making a quick buck on tummy-tucks and face-lifts trumped investing his skill set where it mattered most, in microsurgery, burn reconstruction, and postmastectomy breast reconstruction. With a pot of gold to win at the end of the every aesthetic surgery, he grew disconnected and weary in his work. He was headed toward "irrelevance or death," as Jim Collins describes in *How the Mighty Fall*. Becoming a plastic surgeon sparked a hunger for material wealth and a sincere belief that money was the key to Bill's life satisfaction. The paychecks were big but the benefits were small.

Daniel Pink affirms exactly where material pursuits of this nature have landed many Americans:

> *Abundance has brought beautiful things to our lives, but that bevy of material goods hasn't necessarily made us much happier. The paradox of prosperity is that while living standards have risen steadily decade after*

decade, personal, family, and life satisfaction haven't budged. That's why more people—liberated by prosperity but not fulfilled by it—are resolving the paradox by searching for meaning.[1]

Bill's life was poised for a plunge, as the more money and affluence he gained the less he felt fulfilled. His plastics patients had wants, not needs, and he had the skill set to placate them. His extrinsic needs were being fed with large sums of money, but his intrinsic needs were left hanging and unfulfilled.

The Dangerous Gap

Bill's journey is a primary example of how a life becomes what I term "unFIT." The gap between his work and his *purpose* caused an unhealthy dissonance. The dissonance caused depression and what Jim Collins calls "capitulation to irrelevance." Bill's work lost personal significance; when his passion evaporated, so did he.

His sudden despair wasn't a momentary lapse of judgment as I once thought, or even the leftovers of career burnout, but the detrimental loss of his *purpose*. Bill's life demonstrated tenacity and achievement, but screeched to a halt at the pinnacle of his career. The carrot-and-stick ideology once believed by many as a successful key to motivation proved a myth. The payout isn't everything. Bill realized it the morning he woke up and the nice cars and seven-figure salary didn't matter anymore. What he needed was a *purpose*; he needed the right FIT.

Bill was good at connecting the dots of achievement from high school to an undergraduate degree and beyond, but at the height of his career came a long pause. He lost the sense of meaning behind it all. Why had he become a doctor? In his work, was there anyone whose life truly hung in the balance? Was there meaning behind his motivation?

Playing golf and feeling depressed in his off-time, Bill had time to think. He realized things weren't always this way. The operating room used to thrill him.

He missed the adrenaline rush from watching live surgery as a biology student at the University of Colorado. Now, even to think of it was intolerable. But he always liked being a miracle worker with a scalpel—seeing the problem and cutting it out to change a life.

His patients seeking elective procedures were high-maintenance and fussy. Going into the office was drudgery. As Bill would later recall, "Doing 90 percent cosmetic surgery was not why I'd gone through sixteen years of college, medical school, two residencies, and a fellowship. I felt like a surgical prostitute listening to whiney patients with too much free time, unrealistic expectations, and too much disposable income. I got burned out, and quit."

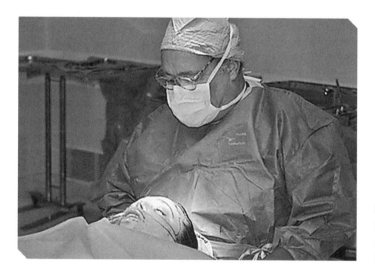

Brother Bill about to do his magic

Bill's early career had been spent in the emergency room treating gunshot victims and people injured in motor vehicle accidents. He saved lives by piecing people together. His specialty in hand and microsurgery reconstruction helped burn patients return to a more normal and fulfilled life. But over time, cosmetic surgery swamped his busy practice.

However, the days of treating burn victims weren't over for Bill—and one whose story pulled him out of his early retirement slump was a woman named Gracie.

Gracie's Story

"Hello, beautiful," Bill greeted the young girl seated in his office. She was all of ten years old, and shifted excitedly in her chair next to her mother. Graciela Nobles was referred to him by the Foundation for Burns and Trauma. Her long-awaited surgery consultation had finally come. She would get a new look—an entirely different face than the one now scarred from her burns.

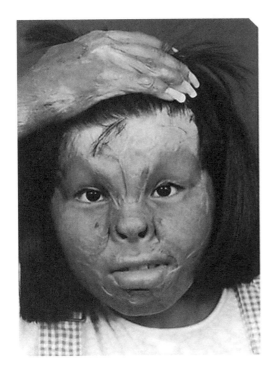

Gracie before finding her FIT with Dr. Leighton

"Dr. Leighton," she asked excitedly, "do you see this little mole up here by my eye?"

"Yes," Bill said, noting also the patchy discoloration and scar lines that landscaped her face. Gracie was young, and her burns hindered that fresh glow owned by so many of her peers.

"Can you move that mole down here?" She pointed to a space just above her lip, implying a beauty mark.

Her mother, Beth Nobles, chided her daughter. "Gracie, don't ask for that!"

"But Dr. Leighton," Gracie persisted, "I want to be a black-headed Marilyn Monroe!"

The girl's wit was a match for Dr. Leighton. "That's all you want?" he asked, his eyebrows flickering in suspense.

She went on to ask for big beautiful lips, a slender nose, and eyebrows slightly higher than they were before.

"We'll do all that and more," he assured her. "And that's going to be in your first surgery."

Gracie's healthy sweep of black hair brushed her round, brown shoulders as she talked excitedly. She wasn't like other patients, stacking cash on the table for breast augmentation or rhinoplasty in an attempt to look like the next magazine celebrity. She was a burn survivor, having been injured when an upended kerosene lamp set fire to her family's hut in a village of the Andes Mountains of Bolivia where she was born.

Gracie's burns went untreated for sixteen days. The pain must have been unthinkable, but she never spoke of it. It was a miracle she survived at all. Gracie's accident was seen as a bad omen in her small village, and her father knew the other villagers would shun her because of it. Fearing for his child's future, he placed her on the back of his motorbike to seek help in the city.

He first took Gracie across the border to seek help from the Chilean government, but as a noncitizen, she was ineligible to receive any benefits. Next he turned to the Bolivian government hospital in La Paz, where Gracie received only two procedures to remedy burns covering 32 percent of her body.

Perhaps more painful than her physical injuries was what happened next. Her father abandoned her, leaving Gracie orphaned.

The orphanage that took her in sent letters to Food for the Hungry, a nonprofit organization that deployed Beth Nobles, an American nurse from Phoenix, to Bolivia. When Beth first met her, Gracie's charm won her over. Beth took the girl back to the United States with a promise to find her a good home. In time, Beth herself adopted Gracie, who was then six years old.

Gracie after working with Dr. Leighton, with her mother, Beth

School pictures were an anticipated event for the other girls, but for Gracie, a deep emotional pain surfaced. Her classmates' questioning looks were damaging her otherwise lively confidence, the very cultural stigma her father hoped she would escape. Beth wanted her new daughter to feel whole, but she struggled to find a surgical option to accept their insurance. With prayer and persistence, Beth sought a plastic surgeon to remedy her daughter's physical scars.

They waited as the years passed. Finally, Beth received a call bearing good news from the Foundation for Burns and Trauma. Dr. William Leighton was opting to complete Gracie's surgery pro bono. Beth described him to Gracie as the "very best" in his field, the surgeon they'd both waited for.

**Gracie and Dr.
Leighton**

Pictures after Gracie's surgery reveal the smooth earth-toned complexion of a young girl with renewed confidence. At a fundraising event for a nonprofit helping to fund other cases like hers, Gracie was the keynote speaker. "I want to say to you, Dr. Leighton, thank you so much," Gracie declared. "I always knew that I looked like this, even as a child, but you peeled back this onion and you unveiled something completely different. I feel like I have a new perspective in life." Now a graduate of Colorado Christian University, Gracie is realizing dreams a little girl from Bolivia never imagined.

In the 1980s, microsurgery had moved to the forefront and surgeons were learning how anything with a blood supply in the body could be reconnected elsewhere. Bill was responsible for pioneering some of the tissue harvesting techniques to aid burn victims, and he honed his specialty in the reattachment of arms, legs, fingers, and toes. Bill was renowned for writing the first research paper on scalp reconstruction and expanding free microvascular flaps for burn patients.

Years later when Dr. Leighton met another burn survivor named Jason, he brought a host of these techniques back into play.

Jason's Story

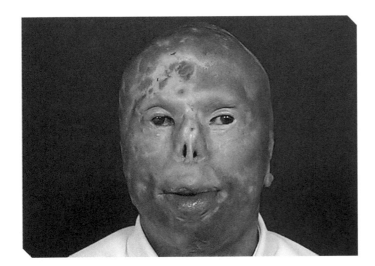

Jason postaccident

Jason's face and hands were heavily disfigured in a fiery car accident that almost claimed his life. He was one of the most resilient men Bill had ever encountered, and after eighteen surgeries they had become close friends.

Jason was a handsome Phoenix police officer one year into the job when his patrol car was rear-ended by a taxi going 115 miles per hour. The taxi driver was experiencing an epileptic seizure at the time of the accident. Jason's car traveled 267 feet through an intersection and caught fire, leaving him unconscious and burning alive inside his Crown Victoria police cruiser.

A fire truck that happened to be only a few blocks away quickly responded, and the firefighters assisted Jason's fellow officers in pulling him from the wreckage. Jason suffered fourth-degree burns on his head, neck, and hands; he credits a bulletproof vest he was wearing with saving his life. In the hospital, Jason's battle for survival continued as the risk of bacterial infection from the damaged tissue threatened his fragile condition. After three months in a medically induced coma and several surgeries to keep Jason afloat, he finally woke up.

Jason had no recollection of the accident, and his wife was the first to tell him what happened. He immediately stopped her from sharing too much. The accident was a cruel kind of irony. Afraid of fire his whole life, Jason never owned a real Christmas tree or a gas BBQ grill to avoid the hazard. His slow trickle of questions to his wife and attending nurse eventually revealed to him the extent of his burns.

The pieces of the puzzle were coming together for Jason, but the road to recovery was long. Jason lost sixty pounds in the hospital as he worked tirelessly to complete physical therapy six months ahead of schedule, learning to eat and walk again. The details of his recovery astounded Dr. Leighton, as he worked to drastically alter the facial scarring. Eighteen surgeries later, he and Jason were routinely exchanging sarcasm and wit despite the long road to reconstruction lying ahead of Jason. Commenting on the doctor's work, Jason choked up with gratitude: "I'm extremely happy when I look in the mirror every day. I'm full of confidence."

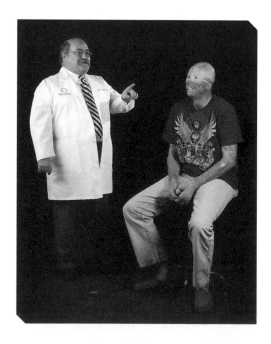

Dr. Leighton and Jason

Jason speaking post–reconstructive surgery

Once Bill had the courage to reexamine his purpose, he found the sense of meaning he'd lost. It wasn't an easy or overnight process, but it worked to bring my brother, a talented physician, back to a role was desperately needed in. If Bill had succumbed to despair and not returned to work, neither Gracie nor Jason would be recipients of these life-changing procedures.

When Bill took time to reevaluate his *purpose*, he realized how his career had veered off course. In opting for aesthetic procedures, his focus shifted toward the extrinsic value of money instead of the intrinsic value of helping others. His elective surgeries provided a large payout, but he was serving a patient population he didn't enjoy working with. He missed the sense of purpose gained in working with burn survivors who'd experienced tragedy and needed a miracle worker. He became "unFIT" and distracted from his goals, forcing him into depression and sudden retirement.

The momentum gained from Bill's rediscovered *purpose* continued with a woman he met at the Houston airport on his way home from a Medical Hands for Healing trip to Nicaragua.

Maribel's Story

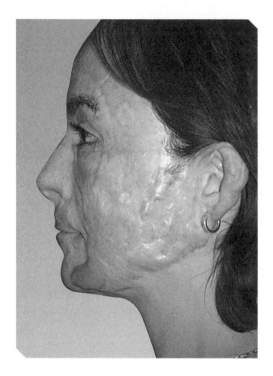

**Maribel
postaccident**

Bill's legacy of helping others continued that day in the airport when he noticed a petite, withdrawn young woman with severe facial burn scars. She was waiting for the same flight Bill was. He introduced himself and asked about the cause of her burns, and was quickly drawn into her story.

One day, at their home in Hermosillo, Mexico, Maribel was in the kitchen with her two sons, ready to start dinner for her family. Her husband, Rudy, was outside unloading their car; they had just returned from a vacation.

In the kitchen, Maribel didn't realize that the gas regulator on the kitchen stove was leaking. When Maribel reached to ignite the stove, it exploded, severely burning her as well as the children.

The children received immediate care at Houston and later at the Shriners Burn Institute in Boston, but Mirabel's condition was too fragile for her to be transported safely from Hermosillo. When she was stable enough to travel, she had been taken to Arizona Burn Center in Phoenix, where she received extensive skin grafting and a tracheotomy, and battled several life-threatening infections. Bill learned that Maribel's insurance wouldn't cover reconstructive plastic surgery in the United States, which explained her severe scarring.

Bill was confident he could find a solution for Maribel, and he asked her to come see him in Arizona. When she arrived, Bill coordinated a team of medical professionals to conduct her surgery pro bono. Rudy and Maribel moved into a small guest house in Tucson for the duration of her long reconstructive process. To express their gratitude, Maribel and Rudy brought homemade food and pastries for Dr. Leighton's staff on every office visit. For this couple's positive attitude despite their circumstances, Bill nominated Rudy and Maribel for an Overcoming Adversity Award through the Jason Schechterle Beyond the Flames Foundation, with a gift of $20,000.

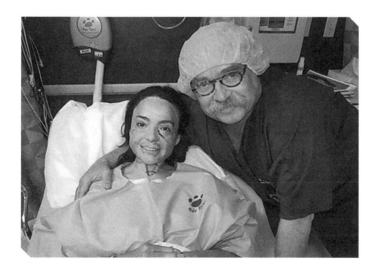

Dr. Leighton and Maribel

Success is understanding the intrinsic value of what we're doing, not necessarily the rewards that appear on the fringe. The FIT framework impacted maximum change in Bill's life, the kind that all the money in the world couldn't accomplish for him. Because he took a moment to reconsider his purpose, he emerged a better and more respected physician than ever.

Psychologist Viktor Frankl claims that pursuing some goal or task for its own sake is the precursor to success:

> *Don't aim at success—the more you aim at it and make it a target, the more you are going to miss it. For success, like happiness, cannot be pursued; it must ensue, and it does so only as the unintended side-effect of one's dedication to a cause greater than oneself.* [2]

Bill admits that a schedule choked with elective surgeries provided little time for altruistic work. But when he invested in the lives of his patients, an influx of awards and esteem followed.

I've never been one to believe product gimmicks or guarantees of "100 percent satisfaction," but I can say that becoming a *Fully Integrated Individual* has accelerated my brother's career in transformational ways. In Bill's acceptance speech for his 100 Club of Arizona Lifetime Achievement Award, he had this to say: "Each and every first responder in this room and the state of Arizona deserve this honor a lot more than I do.... I'm not really sure why you're honoring me for doing something that I absolutely love to do." Those are the words of a man who honors his team first as well as his purpose.

Sometimes, the more financially appealing option isn't always the right option—or, as I like to express it, *the right thing to do is usually the harder of two options*. If we learn how to close the wrong doors and to focus on the right ones, we'll come to a clearer realization of our *purpose*. This includes knowing when to say no to a good thing.

Our focus is easily undermined with too many options, as author Dan Ariely suggests:

> *What we need is to consciously start closing some of our doors.... We ought to shut them because they draw energy and commitment from the doors that should be left open—and because they drive us crazy.*

Transitioning to pro bono reconstructive work was the harder right thing for Bill to do—but it put him back in the game.

When Chris Fenwick, the executive director of the Arizona Institute for Breast Health, happened to run into one of Bill's nurses, Bill learned how many breast cancer patients were left deformed by their treatments. Almost immediately, he began doing breast reconstruction surgeries to make them whole again. Bill also joined the Arizona Institute for Breast Health medical board, which provided free multispecialty expert consultations to women battling breast cancer.

Bill's empathy for his patients earned him recognition as one of "America's Most Compassionate Doctors" in a survey of 7,200 medical practices in the U.S. Bill continues to excel as an instructor for University of Arizona's plastic surgery residency program. Twice he made the University of Arizona College of Medicine dean's list for excellence in teaching in the clinical sciences, an award granted to the top six of 480 clinical faculty members.

Bill's return to practice and his achievements since then can be summarized by this simple statement of his: "I needed to do what I was good at."

A law of physics states that with every action there's an equal and opposite reaction. Bill had to apply the effort to witness the change, as with any good thing in life. I knew I couldn't do it for him, though I daily urged him to reconsider his retirement. This was a hard-fought process for him, and one that required grit.

Finding Your Way Again

There are so many recipes for success available to those seeking to improve their life—yet so few begin with helping them define their *purpose* and *principles*.

Bill's story is a demonstration that FIT helps individuals and the organizations they're part of to achieve and sustain greatness. It shows how easy it is to lose our way—and how to find it again even when we do. It's an essential step to help people and organizations start off on the right foot.

Fallout will come in the process of determining your purpose and committing to it. Some priorities will have to go, and some doors will need to close. This is natural and good, and not easy. Critics may disagree with your level of commitment, especially those lacking the gumption to match it. The reward isn't immediate, and not everyone will agree, but to be a step closer to your *purpose* is to be a step closer to sustainable success, the success of becoming FIT.

Chapter Four
Your Story: Forming Your FIT

I've likened the FIT process to building a house. A house can incorporate many different designs and elements, but the foundation always comes first. And a house is never really finished; though it may appear complete, there's always maintenance and upkeep on the building. Likewise, the FIT process is not static, but invites change as a response to the new challenges and demands of leadership.

PURPOSE → PRINCIPLES → PEOPLE → PROMISE → PLACE

The Five Steps of FIT

In this structure, we steady our foundation with our *purpose*. Then we build its walls with our *principles*, with other *people*, with *promise*, and with a *place*—

in that order. After the structure's built, it can shift and change as a house would adapt to the dynamics within.

Reconnecting with a sense of purpose is something both companies and individuals pursue. It's estimated we spend 25 percent of our lives at work, so it's about time work became something more than what Studs Terkel called a "Monday-to-Friday sort of dying." I've encountered so many unhappy people who quit their jobs years ago but still show up at their workplace. Both the organization and the individual fail to recognize the danger in this.

Anyone—whether fresh out of college, midcareer, or changing lanes on the fast track—has the power to come alive at work and apply FIT. They just need a little help to do it.

FIT begins with questions like these: If you could be your ideal self at work (yes, even in that place you may right now be trying to mentally avoid), *what would that look like?* What would it feel like? What would it mean to you and those around you?

It's time to cast your vision, your mission, and your values to form your FIT—and to shape you, your team, and your organization's future.

Core Questions

Let's begin to map out your purpose for life and work by jotting it down on a piece of scratch paper, or opening up a fresh Word document, or plunking it out on your iPad notes. This is how great ideas begin. Focus on your current state in life and where you want to be in the future. We end up in the wrong position for our skill set or partnered with the wrong people because we've raced past this step. But it's not too late now. Don't be afraid to be ambitious about your future. This isn't sacrificing reality, but shaping it.

Begin your thinking by answering the following basic questions:

1. *Why?* What is your *purpose*—the reason you get out of bed for work in the morning and stay up late at night? Your purpose is defined by the problems

you dream up solutions for. It's your reason for being and the foundation upon which Fully Integrated Teams are constructed. *Actions in your life stem from your purpose.*

Both individuals and organizations have a purpose. Mother Teresa's purpose was to demonstrate love to the poorest population in India. Disney's purpose is to make people happy. We all have a purpose. The clearer it is, the better we'll operate from it in everything we say and do. It's our North Star.

2. *How?* This question helps you identify your *principles,* which are your sense of purpose guided through behavior. It's the means by which your organization or team's purpose is shared with others. Nordstrom's principles are communicated with its "no questions asked" return policy; customer satisfaction is a primary value, and the company asks that every team member participate in accepting returns with a gracious attitude.

3. *Who?* This is about identifying *people*—your Fully Integrated Team—those people whose passions closely align with your purpose. They're contributors who help build FIT with their own solutions, skill sets, and passions. It's also the organization's responsibility to meet or exceed the expectations and needs of its people. Next to *purpose*, getting the right *people* on board is the most crucial step in building a FIT team.

4. *What?* This ultimately has to do with the *promise*—not just the tangible product of an organization or individual, but what is the uniquely relevant value or service provided to others. Perdue promises an enhanced quality of life for everyone it serves through innovative food products; Giorgio Armani promises high fashion designer goods; Phil Mickelson promises a masterful performance in golf.

The *product* is often mistaken for the *promise*, but they're not the same thing. It's easy to get hyperfocused on what comes off the conveyor belt, resulting in actions that disconnect the ends from the means. Be clear with your team's *promise* and understand that it will only be as strong as the *purpose* which drives the organization.

5. *Where* and *When?* This is about *place*. It's where and when your *promise* is delivered, and how the FIT process unfolds in time and space. This the *environment* in which your people are expected to succeed. Creating a sense of place develops culture that will either nourish or destroy your team's productivity. Place is the context that frames your team's success.

FIT Is the Future of Leadership

Starting with the *purpose* might seem counterintuitive, even crazy. Type A leaders want to create something fast and see immediate results from their ideas, so they rush headlong into measuring progress and checking off deadlines. They want a product more than they want a reason for the product. But this is unsustainable.

Jim Collins reminds us of the increasing urgency for today's companies to identify the *reason* behind what they're doing:

> *Confronted with an increasingly mobile society, cynicism about corporate life, and an expanding entrepreneurial segment of the economy, companies more than ever need to have a clear understanding of their purpose in order to make work meaningful, and thereby attract, motivate, and retain outstanding people.*[1]

Warren Bennis echoes that kind of thinking:

> *American organizations (and probably those in much of the rest of the industrialized world) are under-led and over-managed. They do not pay enough attention to doing the right thing, while they pay too much attention to doing things right.*[2]

The purpose is the starting point, period. An organization's *purpose* and *principles* then become the crux of the consumer's decision about whether to do business with a particular company. People attuned with their *purpose* will offer products reflective of the group's collective passion and hard work. This kind of motivation brings forth some of the best products and services available on the market.

So the FIT process works with the established *purpose,* followed by *principles*, *people*, *promise*, and *place*. It's a process that helps move a company or individual toward a desired future state. Once this vision or desired future state is defined, working from the future back toward the present brings the process to life.

The twenty-first century is a bold and exciting era to be working in. With FIT as a framework to lead, guide, and follow, workplaces where passions are being realized are more than possible. FIT is the tool kit that equips organizations and the people within them to achieve and sustain their desired state. FIT teams have fun—because good leaders and educators understand the importance of accomplishing something remarkable together: the power of touching a common nerve.

Building from Purpose

Most people and organizations start their day with questions of *what*: What do I need to accomplish today? What's on my grocery list, my wish list, my to-do list? Few of us start our day with purpose-centered questions: Why am I doing what I do? Why do we as an organization exist?

Pull out your daily planner and browse your days chock-full of detailed whats, wheres and whens—are you aware that you should always begin with the *reason* for those pursuits?

Without secure grounding in our *purpose,* our lives lose their point of reference. Sometimes the very question can send us running for distractions to avoid the answer. We're all haunted by the fear that our lives lack meaning. But with a defined purpose, this fear is easily overcome.

Few leadership experts evaluate what makes for a great leader or organization by beginning with purpose. Most are too focused on getting the right people or delivering a successful promise. Both of these are important factors, but they're not starting points. The *reason* behind a company's existence, or for a doctor operating, or for a product selling, always comes first. This is what differentiates FIT from many other leadership models.

Making Your "Dash"

We live in a world where we need others to help us reach solutions and become better versions of ourselves. Author Jonah Lehrer describes it this way: "Because we live in a world of very hard problems—all the low-hanging fruit is gone—many of the most important challenges exceed the capabilities of the individual."

The low-hanging fruit doesn't require a helping hand or a whole lot of grit to reach, and it's not what FIT people are after in life. We all long for a good challenge and the partnership of great teammates. Accomplishment is about more than just personal goals, but also advancing a legacy where others can finish strong in their own race. Reaching for a goal is not just a physical act, but one of a believing heart. Someone who believes makes his professions public. If you're serious about accomplishing or changing something, let someone know.

Daniel Pink challenges us to define our lives in one sentence or phrase. For JFK it was "to put a man on the moon." For Steve Jobs it was "to put a dent in the universe." Mine is "to serve others while helping them create and reach their desired state through FIT." What's your sentence? I recommend you share it with your spouse or your best friend, someone who'll consistently support you. Make it known and empower your vision into reality.

DEFINING YOUR DASH

Defining Your "Dash"

As I write this book at fifty-six years of age, there's nothing I can do to change how I lived in the past. But I can create what's left of my sentence. Born in 1956, I will die sometime within this century. When all is said and done, the dates on either side of my dash will not define me. It's the dash between that people will remember!

Don't let circumstances dictate the rest of your life, and don't let negative thinking grab hold. Don't allow yourself to fall into the trap of having a victim mentality where hopelessness rules the day. Your life is the summation of your thoughts manifested in your actions by your decisions. The future is yours. Take hold of that gift and never let go.

To borrow from Joseph Addison, there are three essentials to happiness:

1. Something to do.

2. Something (or someone) to love.

3. Something to hope for.

As my mentor Greg reminds me, one enemy of excellence is isolation. Someone to love is vital for emotional and spiritual fitness, as confirmed by leading health experts. Dr. Mehmet Oz admits that he'll operate only on a patient who has someone waiting for them when they come out of the operating room. "I now insist that my patients identify one person who they love and loves them back," he says. "Because if you don't have a reason for your heart to keep beating, then it won't."

Dr. Oz is communicating the *purpose* of each human's existence. Without love, life is devoid of meaning and dreams are a remote possibility. Community gives us purpose as individuals. It's our basic reason to live. We all lack the power to do great things alone, and leaders especially need a supportive "home team."

Daughter Lauren, wife Fritzi, son Jimmy, and me at Sunset Grille enjoying life

The Fully Integrated Teams operate in concentric circles, with family first.

Defining which team members belong in each concentric circle of your life means also ruling out who does not. Invite in only the guests you want to have dinner with. Negative people and circumstances will drain your energy fast. Relationships take time, but they also give it, offering reward and partnership for the journey of life ahead.

Many overworked CEOs and executives assume the "Atlas mentality," believing that the universe rises and falls with the burdens upon their shoulders. For this reason, Greg helps me focus on priority management instead of time management. We can spend a lot of wasted time and energy doing things that don't matter even if the time doing them is managed well. This makes good sense to me, as life can easily be consumed by so many unnecessary details and commitments. As a person who's endlessly curious, always dreaming up solutions and desiring progress, I find that rest is crucial for my leadership.

FIT Under Construction

The FIT House

FIT is a dynamic and engaging journey with the end goal of reaching our desired state as individuals and companies. In many ways it's like undergoing construction in the exchange of old patterns and ways of thinking for more efficient ones.

Like a construction site, with FIT there's never a shortage of work to do. Plans don't always come off perfectly and flexibility is required to keep up with the shape-shifting of the FIT structure. But the joint venture is always exciting and worth the risk!

Much like a builder doesn't arrive on the job site without the necessary materials, we must take inventory of the tools and labor required to achieve our goals and conquer obstacles. What raw materials will each FIT member bring to the table? Which tools will be used in the process to make this structure outstanding? And what hazards on the job must we avoid?

Before the hammer drops on your FIT house, assess these key areas of your FIT job site:

- *Pick the right lot*—a nutrient-rich environment where you can grow.
- *Assess hazards*—energy vacuums and unFIT team members.
- *Assemble raw materials*—needs, skills, and passions.
- *Delegate*—rally passionate people for your Fully Integrated Team.

To help you with these assessments, in the next section of this book we'll get a firm grasp on all the FIT essentials.

Part Two

Growing in FITness

Chapter Five
The FIT Framework

I stated earlier that FIT comes alive at the point where a person's *needs, skills,* and *passions* intersect. Let's zero in on this all-important intersection.

The Flow

My wife and I live in Berlin, Maryland, very close to the ocean. The quaint brownstone shop fronts along Main Street are a respite for many visitors who flock to its small-town appeal. Scenes from the 1999 movie *Runaway Bride,* starring Julia Roberts, were filmed here. But our favorite local spot is just off the beaten path at a great little bar along the inlet harbor. Harborside is the perfect place to loosen up and enjoy good music around some familiar faces. My wife and I like a table just off the main stage where the waiter, Keith, greets us. We know his name, and he knows our food and drinks.

Harborside's stage hosts local talent beneath the bare-bulb lighting in the rafters. One of our favorite bands, Under the Outhouse, has a guitar player named Chris Button. Watching Chris play his guitar is just about the most natural thing I've ever seen. He does it without thinking—the best kind of talent, where skill is channeled without consciousness of the movement.

Unless he drinks too many shots offered by the local patrons, he continues in a daze of play, uninhibited by the world around him. Part of me wonders what Chris does during the day. Is he holding down enough gigs to make ends meet? Is he working a couple of jobs to play in the evenings? How many years has he practiced guitar? These kinds of questions separate the good from the great, even at the local bar.

Chris is tapping into something psychologist and author Mihaly Csikszentmihalyi refers to simply as "flow": a state of effortless concentration and enjoyment while immersed in a particular activity. Doing what fulfills us is the hallmark of FIT, and those who actively practice their passions know it best. The Chris Buttons of the workforce defy doubts that their passions can turn a profit. Their advanced skill sets—borne of long, hard practice hours—prove they have something great to offer.

The idea of work as a necessary evil is obsolete. Work in this context is a natural rhythm that ebbs and flows with purpose. It isn't a means to an end, but when done right, a way of life.

What's Fulfilling About Work?

Work as a reward is an idea that's trickled down from the Puritan Protestant communities that settled in America in the seventeenth and eighteenth centuries. Some of these sects revered work as an act meriting salvation, an approach that led to rigorous if not compulsive productivity. Surely there were those who resented work because of this, though even German sociologist Max Weber considered the benefits in his visit to the United States at the dawn of the twentieth century.

Explaining Weber's view, sociologist Stephen Kalberg writes:

Wherever the spirit of capitalism reigned, work was perceived as a noble and virtuous endeavor; one who engaged in it was respected throughout the community and believed to be of good character. Work played a central role in the formulation even of a person's sense of dignity and self-worth.

Well, there you have it—self-discipline, care of neighbors, and a generally productive society are all factors that led to the Industrial Age, a time when a young nation came alive and entrepreneurs found their pluck. From its primitive beginnings to its modern ends, we can appreciate this period in American history for the grit it has formed within us.

Modernity now pressures us not just to find work, but to find *meaning* in it.

Just ask Srikumar Rao, a professor at Columbia Business School. His wildly popular MBA course "Creativity and Personal Mastery" had its own alumni association for the throngs of students seeking happiness in their career path. He explains why this is so important:

> *I believe that if you don't derive a deep sense of purpose from what you do, if you don't come radiantly alive several times a day, if you don't feel deeply grateful at the tremendous good fortune that has been bestowed on you, then you are wasting your life. And life is too short to waste.*[1]

A life *not* wasted is one that brings *needs, skills,* and *passions* together in a blended alignment.

Let's look closer at each one of those ingredients.

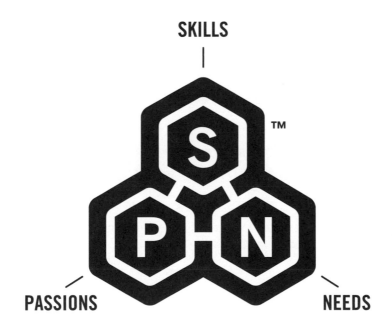

FIT Model

Needs

In many ways, we're all born with needs to express creativity and relate to others in accomplishing things we could never do alone.

There's an important distinction between two different kinds of needs that fulfill us in the workplace or in pursuit of a goal. These needs are iterated by Daniel Pink as *extrinsic* and *intrinsic*.

The intrinsic needs are the key ingredient in what motivates us at work—it's the need closest to our purpose. Intrinsic needs are the real reason we do what we do, and without it, we're just collecting a paycheck—which, as my brother's story demonstrates, is an unsustainable way to live. Bill's greatest intrinsic need was doing what he was good at, and through that, fulfilling the needs of others.

For this reason, when we consider any potential future career, it's absolutely crucial that our intrinsic needs are met or will exceed the extrinsic compensations offered us. Some call this *finding your vocation*.

I'm reminded here of W. H. Auden's observation:

> *You need not see what someone is doing to know if it is his vocation; you have only to watch his eyes; a cook mixing a sauce, a surgeon making a primary incision, a clerk completing a bill of lading, wear the same rapt expression, forgetting themselves in a function. How beautiful it is, that eye-on-the-object look.*

What about your own sense of vocation, and your own intrinsic and extrinsic needs? What have you already discovered about yourself in that regard?

Skills

Vocation is an intrinsic motivation characterized by a deep need to express a particular *skill* set and to share the results with others. Occupations may shift and job descriptions change—but vocation is unchanging. It's closely related to our individual purpose.

The FIT toolbox is the concept of selecting one tool or trade and mastering it. The Amish have a particular affinity for the hammer, as many Amish are builders by trade. It's even said that the right forearm of an Amish man is larger than the left, due to the number of times he swings a hammer. In a similar way, what signature characteristic do others know you by? Is it your ability to initiate conversation, or to energize others and get people going? What is your stand-out area of strength?

Pay attention to your strengths that are pointed out by those who know you well. Look beyond face value at their statements to see what's consistently recognized about your talent. If someone tells you, "You would make a great teacher," while another person says, "You know, I really see your skill set being used as a counselor," note the kind of strengths shared in both professions.

What strengths are others helping you to identify, and how can these shape the future you're creating? Just as a hammer aids a craftsman's ultimate vision of an heirloom trunk, your occupation is a means to accomplish your purpose. Occupation is the tool, and your purpose is the vision behind it.

A tool by itself creates nothing—it's *vision* that drives what the tool can accomplish.

Identifying Your FIT Skill Set

Let these questions help you identify your FIT skill set:

Skill Set: What am I naturally good at? Where do I find energy?

Capabilities: What am I not yet skilled at, but capable of learning to do or to be?

Occupation: How can I monetize my passion while maximizing my meaning?

Vocation: How does this skill set serve my purpose, as well as the purpose of others?

Most of us are really good at only one thing, and after finding this one thing, applying it. But meeting the minimum thresholds of our weaknesses is a prerequisite in most job settings. Once we learn our strengths, we need to be flexible and grow even in our weaknesses.

Creating Your FIT Assessment

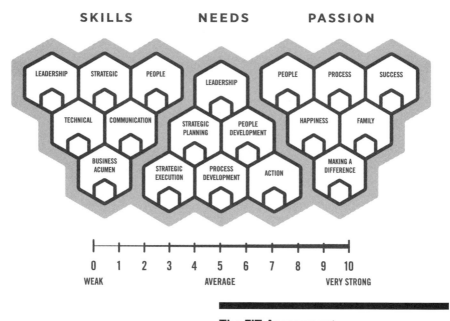

The FIT Assessment

The FIT Assessment is a useful tool in achieving optimal and sustainable FIT. Follow the steps below to determine your correct FIT at the intersection of needs, skills, and passions. Keep in mind not just your own needs as you move thought the model, but also the needs of the organization.

Step 1: Examine the needs pyramid. Rate the importance of each organizational need and place accordingly. For example, an organizational need might be "leadership".

Step 2: Complete the skills pyramid using the same format as the needs pyramid. Rank your vocational skills by level of importance.

Step 3: Rank passions using the same format as indicated in the first two pyramids.

Step 4: Idetify the places where needs, skills, and passion intersect.

Step 5: Add up your score. This will provide you with a strong and useful assessment of FIT with a particular organization.

Passion

At the crossover of needs and skills is where the third important piece of the FIT model intersects: *passion*.

Identifying my own passion happened later in life than it did for my sister Anne. By the age of twelve, a love of music consumed her as she found her "flow" playing the flute and the piano. Teaching music was the clearest path for her future, yet she agonized at the thought of struggling to make an income.

Most twelve-year-olds aren't quite so preoccupied with the future, but Anne was the meticulous kind. She approached my father for advice, and still recalls what he said: "Sweetie, there's all kinds of money out there. People do all kinds of things for all kinds of money. What's important is that you do what you really love to do and do it well. If you remember that, you won't ever have to worry about money." Anne went on to take his advice and become a prolific music teacher.

Even when the path to our future lies in plain sight, we still need encouragement. So much of life is opportunity in those hidden moments, at the crossroads where we stand and decide what will shape us. Money was never the compelling factor in my father's work beyond providing for the needs of his family. Money didn't bring him meaning; *people* did.

When I finished high school, shortly after being declared a future bus driver or ditch digger, I assumed work as a card-carrying laborer. My good friend John Armstrong and I joined the union in search of a higher paid seven-dollar-an-hour gig. We arrived at the labor hall in Marseilles, Illinois, a fifteen-minute drive from Ottawa. The labor hall was a run-down place full of people waiting to get called to a work site.

There was a bar next to the labor hall where, to my amazement, my coworkers found refuge in the early morning hours. One morning we were called to work and asked to pick up another member who'd already spent too much time in the bar. After we clocked him in to his work site, we dropped him off at the boneyard to sober up.

Our first job was digging holes for the foundation of a building. We cleared dirt around cement structures that we would later extract with the use of jackhammers. My first day, I was digging with vigor when the guy next to me asked, "What are you doing, man?" I thought it was a joke until he voiced his real concern: "Slow down, you're making me look bad!" I'll never forget that remark—so crude and without a hint of shame. I wasn't about to slow down. I wanted to work hard and earn my keep. How could I feel good about myself if I just took it easy, relying on a labor union to protect me?

Another day, while working at a nuclear power plant under construction, one of the laborers had a crane operator lift a hollow cement cylinder over him so he could sleep the day away. It dumbfounded me how hard some men worked at getting out of their work.

This was enough to convince me that only a persistent work ethic led to success in my own life and the lives of others. Author David Novak states it wisely:

> *Your ability to reach your goals has as much to do with how you choose*
> *to see the world as it does with your level of education and intelligence.*
> *And this is totally within your control, because your mind-set is up to you.*

After the day-laborer gig, John and I backpacked around Europe with our two thousand dollars in savings. We visited seven countries in two months and had a blast. After returning, I followed up on a phone call I'd received from the swim coach of Carthage College in Kenosha, Wisconsin. Earning a college degree now meant that I could spend the rest of my life being in a place I enjoyed doing something I actually loved. I leapt at the opportunity. I accepted his offer to swim for their team and to study at Carthage my first two years of college. It was there that I also reignited my pursuit of golf, winning MVP both years on the Carthage team.

A successful stint at Carthage left me wanting a greater challenge. My friend John attended the University of Iowa, and a bigger school meant greater opportunities, so I transferred there. Arrangements were made by my Kenosha golf coach to meet with the University of Iowa golf team to have lunch and for me to play a round as a walk-on. Seated at their table after one nerve-wracked round, I felt dwarfed by the skill level of my colleagues. One of the players was Guy Boros, the son of famous PGA golfer and Hall of Famer Julius Boros. I struggled to engage them in conversation as I felt my insecurities closing in. The obligatory "nice to meet you's" were exchanged after lunch, and that was it.

I lacked grit, discipline, and belief to elevate my game with a little extra work. At that moment, golf became a friendly hobby instead of a potential vocation. I missed an opportunity to create a desired future in golf. Fortunately, other opportunities came along that I took by the horns. My father always advised me to do what I really loved and to be exceptional at it. Sharing his love for people, it seemed fitting for me to enter the snack foods industry, more specifically Nabisco.

Passion's Defining Moments

Some of us take a more linear path than others. Mine was a fairly direct connect-the-dots journey from high school on through the University of Iowa, though a few defining moments set me on the path to success, thanks to my parents' persistence. One was the intellectual analysis test I mentioned earlier.

Though it was an unpleasant experience, it was memorable. Working as a day laborer cured me of turning into reality that picture of my future as a bus driver or ditch digger.

What are your defining moments? What was the last book you read that completely captivated you? What part of your childhood dream are you living out now? Who did you meet along the way that inspired you and provided guidance for your future career? These questions are important insights into your story, a story with an unfinished ending. Think of each day as a chapter and each moment as a page in the book you're building with your life—a book that your children and friends will read. How would you like your story to read, and what is that story about?

These are questions of *passion*. Passion isn't a whimsical feeling, but a grounded orientation in what consistently fuels our lives with energy. Without it, we lose our focus and become easily depressed.

One of the easiest ways to identify passion is to measure our energy surrounding particular activities. What keeps us up late at night? What problem must we absolutely solve, just for the sake of figuring it out?

You might log your thoughts in any given day, writing down situations that are at the extreme of happiness and frustration. Over a period of time, a trend will emerge on what cues up your passion and what diminishes it.

Another good technique is simply to listen to what others point out about your strengths. When you hear comments like "You're a natural at that" or "You were born to do this," filter those tag words and store them. Ask yourself, "What is it about my performance that they admired?" Connect their insights to your existing knowledge of your strengths and weaknesses. In doing so, you might be in business in a whole new way. An honest outsider can offer the best insight into your natural capacities and strengths.

Ensuring the Best Hires

The FIT model is a two-way street that helps me make informed recruiting choices. The cost of a bad hire damages both team morale and financial resources. The *Harvard Business Review* calculates that as much as 80 percent of employee turnover is due to bad hiring decisions, increasing in cost as the turnover occurs higher up the corporate ladder. The U. S. Department of Labor estimates that it costs a company the equivalent of one-third of the new hire's annual salary to find a sufficient replacement when a turnover occurs.

I always use the FIT model in new-hire interviews. One interview I led for Perdue's senior research and development position demonstrates the power of *FIT* and active listening.

The female applicant conveyed a professional demeanor and was very well-spoken, though a bit nervous at first. Overqualified on the technical side of things, she had both domestic and international experience. But what I really wanted to know was hidden in her life story. As we advanced through the FIT model, her human side emerged.

On a sheet of paper, I sketched for her the FIT model of needs, skills, and passions in three interlocking circles, and explained how this affected our conversation.

"Let's start with the needs circle," I suggested, popping off my first question: "How would Perdue as a company meet your needs, and how would you fulfill Perdue's needs through this opportunity?"

She affirmed that Perdue was a place that demonstrated a passion for her personal success and fulfillment.

We proceeded next to the passion circle, and with her permission, we continued. (I always asked permission to continue with this step, for the comfort of the interviewee. Some candidates are more willing than others to share their dreams, aspirations, and failures; for some, the topic is uncomfortable or personal.)

She said, "I'm passionate about people."

"Why?" I questioned. "Not all people are."

She took a moment to think. "No one has ever asked me that!" she said. "I enjoy seeing people succeed because it makes me feel proud of them."

Again, I asked her why.

As she continued to speak frankly with me, she broke down in tears. Her passion for others' success was directly inspired by her children. She lost three of her six children in pregnancy, prior to birth.

Gathering her composure, she shared how her three living children are the driving passion of her life. They inspire her to care for others with the same overflowing passion. She shared with me examples of how her passion to serve created value for her previous employer. This was a valuable insight that aligned directly with Perdue's reason for being: to enhance people's quality of life.

Your Own FIT Framework

Before going forward, I urge you to go back through this chapter and face up personally to the questions presented here about needs, skills, and passion. Make sure you understand who you are in each of these areas, and clearly articulate what you discover.

Chapter Six
The FIT Mind-Set

In the movie *The Great Escape*, Steve McQueen breaks out of a German prison camp to get caught—on purpose. His aim is to provide other Allied prisoners of war with outside information to benefit their future escape efforts. I'd like to do something similar; I want to provide you the techniques to escape your own mental prison that might be leading you toward an undesirable future state.

In the film, McQueen's character creates a desired future state and plans his great escape accordingly "I haven't seen Berlin yet," he says, "from the ground or from the air, and I plan on doing both before the war is over." He refuses to stay put. You can create your own great escape, but unlike McQueen, you can make it all the way to freedom and well beyond the border of captivity—and stay there. The key to your freedom is visualization.

Successful people demonstrate the will to succeed. They take hold of factors within their control and make them work to their advantage. This process in the mind begins with the five fundamental truths a successful person accepts. Let's look at them, one by one.

Certain Ways of Thinking Are Better Than Others

Everyone wants to win, and some desperately. Yet most people approach winning like a daydream, imagining the reward without creating a disciplined frame of mind to attain it. Our brains are capable of shaping the outcome-winning path to success if we engage them better and more often.

Professional athletes like Michael Phelps and Tiger Woods use visualization techniques to improve their performance. The perfect shot, the flawless stroke, or the winning goal is the result of visualization. Creating a mental picture of the intended result, scene by scene, is a technique that unlocks the hidden strengths and capacities of the mind.

Golf is a mental game. A few years back, I was having a horrible round for a single-digit handicap player. After I'd struggled for a few holes, a friend of mine said to me, "Jim, the hardest hole in golf is the nine inches between your ears." He was right. There are two realities on the course: the actual and the envisioned. The bridge between them is the mind. Every golf shot needs a vision. The more accurate this vision, the better the shot.

When professional Jack Nicklaus envisions his golf shot in his mind's eye, he notes the speed and trajectory of the ball from its current position to its final resting spot. His focus is on nothing but the intended consequences of his actions. He knows he'll hit a great shot. The hazards in front of him are out of his mind; he's avoiding distraction to make his potential a reality.

Now suppose an MRI image is captured of Nicklaus's brain while visualizing his perfect shot, followed by another image captured while he's taking the shot. The two images would look decidedly similar; the same degree of similarity is revealed by MRI scans conducted on subjects who were either envisioning a sunset or actively viewing it. What the mind creates is shockingly close to reality—what we envision and what we do are more connected than we realize.

Visualization is about creating an optimum visual environment for performance, complete with surround sound. A vivid frame-by-frame visualization may trigger memories of recent successes, creating tracks in the brain like footprints in the snow. For a basketball player, it's not enough to just see the ball going into the hoop. He must feel the ball leaving his fingertips, see the arc it travels through the air, and hear the swish of the net.

A study by Australian psychologist Alan Richardson with a group of basketball players shows how this works. Richardson's experiment split up a group of basketball players into three groups. The first group practiced only free throw shots for twenty days; the second only visualized free throw shots for twenty days; the third group neither visualized nor practiced free throws for twenty days. When the data of each group's performances were collected, Richardson found a 23 percent improvement among participants who only visualized for twenty days, just slightly behind the improvements of those who actually practiced free-throw shots.

The power of imagery is an understatement. One of the most remarkable findings in the history of neuroscience is the malleability of the brain. Scientists refer to this property as neuroplasticity. The brain is not a rigid, deterministic structure, but one full of possibility and surprise. This was about as huge a revelation to the scientific community as Galileo's proclamation that the earth revolves around the sun! Genes no longer rule the day or limit our destiny, and the evidence points to our mind as the shaper of success.

In *The Brain That Changes Itself,* author Norman Doidge relates Dr. Antonio Pascual-Leone's "snowy hill" metaphor to illustrate how new neural connections are formed:

> *The plastic brain is like a snowy hill in the winter. Aspects of the hill—the slope, rocks, trees, consistency and depth of the snow—are like our genes, a given. When we slide down the hill on a sled, we can steer it and will end up at the bottom of the hill by following a path determined both by how we steer and the characteristics of the hill. Where exactly we will end up is hard to predict because there are so many factors in play.*[1]

Pascual-Leone goes on to say that "what will definitely happen the second time you take the slope down is that you will more likely than not find yourself somewhere or another that is related to the path you took the first time."

The more often a behavioral sequence is repeated, the stronger the underlying brain circuits become. At some point, the new neural pathways become the brain's default option. It's possible to change negative thoughts over a period of time, though it may take months or even years.

As Daniel Goleman suggests, the emotional center of the brain must practice new behaviors repetitively:

> *The neocortex, the thinking brain that learns technical skills and purely cognitive abilities, gains knowledge very quickly, but the emotional brain does not. To master a new behavior, the emotional centers need repetition and practice.*

It sounds like a lot of work. So why change your thoughts? Because positive thoughts are better than negative ones. When the mind travels a positive thought path, the outcome is always greater. Ridding ourselves of negative thoughts helps us reach our goals, lose weight, and even relax more deeply.

Changing Thoughts Requires Practice

New brain pathways are a bit like wet cement—needing time to solidify. Learning something new requires the discipline of the conscious brain. It's not until we've practiced something again and again that our unconscious brain performs a task without our conscious micromanaging. We must repeat the same behaviors repeatedly until the unconscious monopolizes the process.

It reminds me of a golfer I watched in the Tournament Players Championship. He was leading after fifty-four holes, then his momentum fell apart. He could no longer "pull the trigger" to continue winning; his mind succumbed to the pressure and would not allow his body to hit the ball. Every golfer familiar with the mental rigor of the game knows what was happening to this young man. His audible grunts of frustration elicited my sympathy. His mind was getting in the way. This player's emotional brain centers needed more practice and repetition to land his success.

Deliberate practice is a challenge, both difficult and painful at times. So few of us make it to the top because our lack of commitment and grit caps our ability to succeed. But when we've put in the work, our default mental roads form correct pathways, aligning our willpower toward success.

Positive thinking leads to positive outcomes—down a path of increasing accountability for our actions. We can and should create an envisioned future before waiting for the future to create itself.

Positive thinking guru Martin Seligman coined the term "learned optimism" in the early 1990s. It was a direct counter to the psychological term "learned helplessness," described as an individual's inability to cope with negative circumstances resulting in a characteristic behavior of defeat. Learned optimism leads individuals to success. It's not just a way of thinking, but a way of doing. A study Seligman conducted with new life insurance agents found that the optimistic agents sold 37 percent more in their first two years than their pessimistic counterparts.

Positivity Pays

I had the opportunity to build and manage a fitness facility in one of many office buildings owned by a man named Clement Stone. Clement Stone was an entrepreneur whose rags-to-riches story embodies radical positivity. He and I share a passion for positive thinking that results in tangible success. Stone's path to success resounds so clearly with FIT.

Stone was just three years old in 1905 when his father died. A financial mess of gambling losses was the only inheritance his father left the family, who were already living well below the poverty line. Hardship was a far cry from defeat for Stone, who began selling newspapers at six years old, doing his best to scrape by.

After years of hard survival at a young age, Stone finally made his breakthrough. At sixteen, he started making cold calls selling casualty insurance for his mother's new agency. He had figured out how to make one hundred dollars a week. At age twenty, Stone opened his own insurance company, the beginnings of the Combined Insurance Company of America empire. Habitual positivity and a lot of hard work made Stone a self-made millionaire. In 2002, his obituary appeared in the *New York Times* under this headline: *Clement Stone dies at 100; Built an Empire on Optimism.*

Successful people move on quickly. They don't hold tightly to past successes or mistakes but move in one direction: *ahead.* Unsuccessful people become mired in the past, too focused on what's already taken place to visualize what the future holds. That's one of the reasons successful people learn much faster than unsuccessful people. They don't internalize failure or success. They accept imperfections and pass them off, not just hoping for better next time, but *doing* better. They connect the dots of their own life and don't play the victim of circumstance. To paraphrase Edison in his relentless pursuit of the perfect lightbulb, finding ten thousand ways that don't work just means you're one step closer to the right solution.

Negative Thought Momentum (NEMO) Leads to Failure

There are two kinds of thinking that distinguish those who fail from those who succeed.

The first is NEMO—negative momentum. The way unsuccessful people think doesn't get them where they want to go. Like a broken compass, it points them in the wrong direction along an undesirable slope of habitual behavior. This spiral of habitual negative thought creates negative experiences that deliver an undesirable state of being. The mind familiarizes itself with negativity and becomes the filter through which every thought passes.

Unsuccessful thoughts always lead to unsuccessful choices. Choices are the decisions we make after determining our range of possibilities in reaching a goal. Think of choices as the link between thoughts and actions. We have an almost unlimited inventory of thoughts to choose from, on a broad spectrum ranging from positive (nourishing) to negative (toxic). Most thoughts are somewhere in between, but for the sake of example, we'll deal with the more extreme thoughts leading to failure.

Negative thoughts are inconsistent with our purpose and our stated goals. Our purpose acts as the gatekeeper to ward off any harmful thoughts from damaging our goals. Our self-talk is crucial in how we pursue a goal toward success or failure. Imagine again that golfer in the Tournament Players Championship who fell apart after going strong for fifty-four holes. What did his self-talk sound like as NEMO crept in and took control of his performance? Here's my best guess:

a) "That last shot was terrible. Everybody's watching to see how I screw up next!"

b) "I just bogeyed on that last hole. I'm already too far out of the lead!"

c) "What an embarrassing performance; why am I even here?"

Negative thoughts threaten to overwhelm us. When we meditate on failure, we allow it to define our future. It's plain to see how negative self-talk wouldn't help us reach our goals, yet it's ironic how we allow our own minds to be tripped up with out-of-control pessimism.

In *The Power of Habit,* Charles Duhigg proposes a helpful model to changing our negative thought habits. Based on research conducted at MIT on habit formation, he explains the anatomy of habit as *cue, routine,* and *reward.* Duhigg suggests that preprogrammed reactions to our triggers may cause our habit cycle to kick in, producing the same outcome each time. If our habit is a negative thought pattern, we must analyze what triggers our negative thoughts (cues), and at what times (routine), and with what outcomes (reward), thus causing us to repeat the behavior. Examining our self-talk is one way to preemptively correct our negative thought cycle.

Positive Thought Momentum (POMO) Leads to Success

In his book *Change Your Thinking, Change Your Life,* Brian Tracy appeals to something called the Law of Substitution. It's the idea that the mind has room to house only one thought at a time. If this thought is positive, it has reigning power. If the thought is negative, the same is true. Is your one thought for the day negative? How can it become an opportunity for a positive alternative?

We examined the golfer's thoughts consumed with NEMO. They resulted in poor performance, and, far worse, a behavior that painted failure as normative and success as something out of his control. Now let's image what his self-talk would sound like with POMO at play:

a) "I've had better games, but tomorrow's a new day. I'll beat my last score in the next competition."

b) "That bogey was an exception to the rule; I know I can do better, and I'll show it with my next birdie."

c) "If I play my best now and refuse to give up, I can still finish with a respectable score."

These thoughts detract from our NEMO to leverage it for the positive. Using POMO, we take life one shot at a time, not ignorant of our shortcomings but seeking to develop them.

POMO ultimately drives success. Jim Kilts, business great and former CEO of Kraft, Nabisco, and Gillette, refers to this marvelous phenomenon as inertia. The law of inertia describes how matter continues in uninterrupted motion unless acted on by an outside force. When POMO is the driving force of your life, even something as daunting as terminal illness can be transformed into an opportunity.

From Illness to Opportunity

Eugene O'Kelly, founder and CEO of the KPMG accounting firm, demonstrated the power of POMO for so many when at fifty-three years old he was diagnosed with an aggressive terminal brain cancer. With about a hundred days to live, O'Kelly didn't blissfully ignore his illness, but filled each remaining day with as much life and goodness as it afforded. He also found time to complete a memoir to mentor others on the process of finishing life well.

Shortly after his diagnosis, O'Kelly shared these thoughts:

> *Most people don't get this chance. They're either too sick or they have no clue death is about to happen. I have the unique opportunity to plan this about as well as it can be planned.*

O'Kelly speaks of his impending death as an opportunity—not that it was easy, or that at times it didn't frighten him to his core. He accepted his chance to be fully alive until death, demonstrating POMO not in principle, but in action.

Live your next hundred days with more purpose than the last. Make more than a bucket list out of your life, and actually *do* the things you envision—starting now.

Environment

Everyone from CEOs right down to Little League players operate as connected systems of influence. Our relationships and even our own bodies heed this biological rule of connectedness.

In Bruce H. Lipton's book *The Biology of Belief*, he provides extensive new biological research indicating how DNA is controlled by signals from outside the cell, including the energetic messages emanating from our positive and negative thoughts.

Each of our bodies operates as a cooperative community of approximately fifty trillion cells. Almost all of the cells that make up our bodies are amoeba-like, individual organisms that have adapted a strategy for survival. These cells come together for a greater purpose.

According to Lipton, these cells "actively seek environments that support their survival while simultaneously avoiding toxic or hostile ones. Like humans, single cells analyze thousands of stimuli from the microenvironment they inhabit. Through the analysis of this data, cells select appropriate behavioral responses to ensure their survival."[2]

Through cells, we understand the importance of our *environment*. POMO isn't achieved solely in positive thoughts, but in places, people, and things that nourish the environment in which to live and grow. Environment has a profound influence on how well POMO is sustained. This means the *physical* environment—where one lives, works, and invests free time, and what one eats and drinks; as well as the *social* environment—one's friends and family, hobbies, interests, and passions.

Statistician David Banks cites the influence of environment on success. He notes the close grouping of prodigious artists emerging in Florence, Italy, between 1450 and 1490, including Leonardo da Vinci, Ghiberti, Michelangelo, Botticelli, and Donatello. He further cites the philosophers of Athens between 440 and 380 B.C., including Plato, Pericles, Thucydides, Herodotus, Euripides, and many others. Success was no accident in either of these prolific societies. Beginners partnered with seasoned mentors and masters of their trade to become great.

You and Your Work Environment

The FIT model of Needs, Skills, and Passions shows blank space occupied by the word *environment*. Environment and culture are crucial but often overlooked factors in an individual's success. Think about environment as the water quality within your company—or as *Fast Company* blogger Shawn Parr suggests, as the cleanliness of your "aquarium."

Stagnant water makes the fish die in an aquarium, and stale culture in a company prompts good employees to migrate to more desirable waters. Why?

Because people seek more than a paycheck; they want a holistic, meaning-driven experience at work.

But before you throw the company out with its bathwater, here are three points to consider:

1. What is within my power here to *change*? How can I suggest an update to company culture that will create a mutually desirable environment?

2. Think of employment as a relationship, not a contract. What can you do to contribute better to the relationship? There's a time for both give and take.

3. Assess personal risk. Discern if the water is toxic to your growth within the company. Is it time to seek out a different working environment?

In gauging the health of your work environment, identify energy vacuums. Understand what your team members expect from you if they don't do a good job explaining it. Miscommunication is a common energy vacuum that can leave team members spinning their wheels. Part of your job is finding out your role within any team. Visualize how your work habits and personal style will align or conflict. Ask questions that get at the heart of what the company values most: its people or its bottom line.

Energy Vacuums

Ask yourself these questions:

- How is my work environment feeding my strengths?
- What kind of upward mobility or rewards are available to me?
- What kinds of tasks are particularly stressful for me at work, and how does my workload counterbalance those tasks with ones I enjoy?
- Does my boss demand long hours without opportunities to recharge and rest?
- Does my office environment consider my personal work preferences? If not, is there an option to telecommute for part of the work week?

Removing and neutralizing energy vacuums from our workplace is one of the quickest ways to achieve FIT status and get our energy back. It's all about being present and engaged when we show up for work. Eugene O'Kelly states it this way: "Commitment is best measured not by the time one is willing to give up, but more accurately by the energy one wants to put in, by how present one is."

Passionate and engaged employees investigate potential work environments. They ask questions like these: What skills does this organization have to fulfill my needs? How collaborative and interested are they about serving my extrinsic (compensation) and intrinsic (social and self-actualization) needs?

The latest in productivity theories focus not on hours spent working, but on energy levels of work. The concept of renewable energy isn't just for natural resources; it's for workplaces too. In the article "Manage Your Energy, Not Your Time," authors Tony Schwartz and Catherine McCarthy make this claim: "Most large organizations invest in developing employees' skills, knowledge, and competence. Very few help build and sustain their capacity—their energy—which is typically taken for granted."

Your Own FIT Mind-Set

Once again I encourage you to go back through this chapter and carefully answer the questions it poses. How is your mind-set? Can you identify mental changes and new directions that can free you up for greater fulfillment and FITness?

Chapter Seven
Grit Makes Greatness

In Ernest Hemingway's *The Old Man and the Sea,* Santiago is a poor, weathered fisherman with a strike of bad luck. His fellow Cuban villagers mock him for his plight, and even his young business partner has abandoned him. After eighty-four days without a catch, everyone expects Santiago to surrender to fate and spend the rest of his days on land. But the man perseveres.

On the eighty-fifth day, Santiago prepares his lines with the same meticulous expectation as before. The villagers mock him, but he carries on. He rows his skiff further than ever into the Gulf of Mexico—and there he hooks a miraculous catch, an eighteen-foot marlin. He struggles against the giant fish for three exhausting days until it finally gives in. Unable to land his monstrous catch in the skiff, Santiago battles sharks devouring his trophy fish in the water. He beats them back with oars, but is left with only a carcass by the time he rows into port. Despite his discouraging circumstances, Santiago remains hopeful to fish another day.

In this short novella, Hemingway depicts the resilience of the human spirit. At times I've felt like Santiago, unable to catch a break, let alone a fish. Santiago is an example of the kind of person I want to be even in the midst of failure. He had nothing but bloodied hands and a fish skeleton to show for his battle, yet he won the war on defeat. He chose hope.

Tapping into Your Resilience

We all have this miraculous will to overcome. We champion stories like Santiago's because we all know what it's like to have a showdown with the sharks—when the road gets rough, and we have to use our grit. Santiago may have lost the battle for his dinner, but he never lost his fighting spirit.

Grit is the resilience of an individual in the face of real or perceived obstacles and setbacks along the way toward personal success. It's part of the nature of a fighter who's had enough beat-downs to teach him how to outwit his opponent. It's the will to overcome an obstacle, and it's the only reason the lightbulb and many other modern conveniences were invented. It's that persistent voice in my head that believed I'd be more than a ditch digger. (It turned out to be right.)

Grit means enduring years of obscurity. It means hard work without reaping immediate payoff. It means patient obedience to the future without immediate gratification of the present. In his book *Outliers: The Story of Success,* Malcolm Gladwell asserts that it takes roughly ten years or 10,000 hours of practice to master a skill set. It's an assertion based on research by neurologist Daniel Levitin, who wrote: "In study after study of composers, basketball players, fiction writers, ice skaters, concert pianists, chess players, master criminals, and what have you, this number comes up again and again."

Greatness is not a microwave phenomenon, but a slow, painful refinement. Or to paraphrase Thomas Edison, we miss opportunity because it looks like work. Nothing trumps good old-fashioned hard work. People with grit don't look for shortcuts. Persistence (along with a few other things) transforms raw skill into mastery. Greatness is more than a lofty notion; greatness demands grit.

Expect Failure

Grit brings to mind pictures of the old American frontier, of pioneers and their resolve. It also evokes images of mountaineers and extreme sports junkies rising to the top of their game, some even dying to get there. It's the stuff of injuries and setbacks, and it sometimes receives the mockery of others.

Although it might seem counterintuitive, I believe that the best people—the most perfectionist, overachieving kind—expect to face failure at some point in life. This is what makes them the best. They plan for it, so that when it comes, it will be a minor setback instead of a mountain of defeat. All great people have failed, some monstrously. Yet there's something visceral and human that spurs us on to know unprecedented success through perseverance.

Former President Teddy Roosevelt suggested that if we aren't striving toward something greater than ourselves, we've already failed. He pictured a patient boxer—

> *...the man who is actually in the arena, whose face is marred by dust and sweat and blood; who strives valiantly; who errs, who comes short again and again, because there is no effort without error and shortcoming; but who does actually strive to do the deeds;...who spends himself in a worthy cause; who at the best knows in the end the triumph of high achievement, and who at the worst, if he fails, at least fails while daring greatly.*[1]

Learning from Failure Breeds Grit

My father used to tell me that getting an education in life is never cheap. There's a certain wisdom gained from grit experiences, the kind I learned in full after my own brush with failure.

I started my first company as an idealistic twenty-one-year-old college graduate. I built National Health Management Company from the ground up, then sold it the day before I got married—now thirty years ago. I agreed to show the new owners the ropes by staying on with the business for another year. When the year was up, I turned down an attractive equity position they offered me, and instead moved to California to start a new business venture.

With proceeds from the sale of my business burning a hole in my pocket, I bought a Porsche—not exactly a wise investment, but an impulse buy that suited our move to California. My new wife and I filled the moving truck with goods from our Illinois apartment and drove west until we reached the Pacific.

My new business partner was someone I knew from high school. John and I invested in a series of high-end private training facilities called Matrix One in Westwood, California. That quickly became the biggest mistake of my young career. The management's lack of good business sense came with a hefty price tag.

The concept was lavish and drew in a movie star clientele, including Tom Selleck, Tatum O'Neal, Randy Jackson, and even Arnold Schwarzenegger. An article from *People Magazine* described the layout as "an aerobics room with special floor padding prescribed by an orthopedic surgeon, a state-of-the-art Questar weight room outfitted with water-resistant machinery, a Nautilus room for traditionalists, and for those who earn a living from looking good, a tanning room, a hair salon, and pink track lights to give exercisers a graceful glow when they happen to glance in the wall-to-wall mirrors."[2]

With a lot of PR buzz, we broke ground on our second facility in Beverly Hills. A site was selected, plans were drawn, and preopening memberships were secured.

Then, back in Illinois, I received a phone call from John. The site selected for the Beverly Hills location had some zoning issues related to our use of the property.

John and his team quickly found another site and began construction with virtually no planning. The award-winning facility featured in *Architectural Digest* cost almost double what we had forecast in our budget. Our strategy was fast and loose, pampering the influx of celebrity clients while bluffing the company's bottom line.

Budgets were managed loosely in the construction of our second facility, and I learned how celebrity clientele were simply given memberships to work out there. When John called me up to champion our million-dollar revenue figures, I sobered him with the reality that our runaway spending far exceeded any profit we'd made. Gaining business acumen was very expensive in this case.

Lack of good execution eventually surfaced. Just two years after Matrix One launched, John went bankrupt after I pulled the plug on the overspending. I lost every penny of my hard-earned investment. We were too focused on the immediate without investing in the company's future. It was a race to make a quick buck, and the company's momentum burned up prematurely.

The Comeback Kid

Denial of the brute facts summoned a Chapter 7 bankruptcy for Matrix One. I failed to see this collapse until it was imminent. Matrix One dropped off the radar like a Hollywood hopeful in her dazzling ten seconds of fame. Those hired to run the business had too much fun with the money, and now it was gone: all gone. I didn't see a penny on the investment I made, as I was barely able to cut a check for the remaining employees.

This was a moment of insight. I had trusted the wrong *people,* and I had largely underestimated what they were capable of. Without a clear *purpose,* I had thrown my hard-earned money at an exciting business gamble, only to watch it go sideways.

I face that egg-shaped number of defeat each time I see the earnings category in my annual Social Security statement. To give up was never an option—so I chalked up my loss as a very expensive life lesson, and I moved forward.

As author Diane Coutu affirms, learning to be *resilient* is the key to future success:

> *Resilient people possess three characteristics: a staunch acceptance of reality; a deep belief, often buttressed by strongly held values, that life is meaningful; and an uncanny ability to improvise. You can bounce back from hardship with just one or two of these qualities, but only with all three will you be truly resilient.*[3]

Determining FIT is important for more than just good business sense. Without it, we lead lives of aimless wandering, trying vainly to make things work when situations, people, or relationships are misaligned. Our mode of operation must change from grasping for dollar signs to a FIT definition of success. I like Simon Sinek's definition: "Success comes when we wake up every day in that never-ending pursuit of WHY we do WHAT we do."

The Success Quotient

The Success Quotient is something that leverages natural intellect, emotional aptitude, and grit. It demonstrates how individuals are propelled into lasting success. Be selective in applying the success quotient. Do not try to be the best of everthing; try to be the best in the world at one thing.

Here it is: *IQ + EQ + GQ = Success.*

The Intelligence Quotients (IQ) refers of course to an individual's natural intellectual capacity or know-how. The Emotional Quotient (EQ) is a combination of one's self-awareness and empathy. The Grit Quotient (GQ) is the zeal by which setbacks and failure are overcome.

These three are necessary to succeed. When the minimum threshold for IQ and EQ are met, grit is what carries us through to the end.

Daniel Pink claims that the world is littered with intelligent, talented people who are lacking this key ingredient to success. Why? They simply refuse to exert the effort to do something truly remarkable. Pink says, "Doggedness trumps talent and intellect almost every time." It's true.

FIT to Thrive

Grit is a force that shows up when our determination is to not just survive, but to thrive. For both organizations and individuals, we thrive as we become FIT.

We know that life isn't meant to be lived halfway, and our souls answer with a longing for more—more meaning for our work, more zest for life, more energy in a day, and more inspiration. Good enough is not enough; we want happiness, contentment, and the kind of success that *means* something. Like a garden, we want to see new growth, not just a seed in the ground.

When you're just getting by—whether in a relationship or your finances—it's a means-to-an-end way of life with no longevity. It's this kind of behavior that's to blame for our discontentment and yearning for more. If there's an unfulfilled dream sitting on the back burner of your life, now is the time to stop ignoring it.

Harnessing the intrinsic motivations and passions of every worker is crucial in the workplace. Individual strengths are abundant as ever, but those who are good at developing them are few. The strengths of our teams determine the future of our organizations. Understanding the universal need for personal fulfillment is paramount. Activating that need, growing it, and finding a way to express it for the benefit of the team is the next step.

Empathy is a quality that I personally seek to grow in. Empathy is the ability of a leader to engage and empathize with the emotions (EQ) of others. It's also a success-driver in the workplace. A hallmark of empathy is possessing good listening skills, or, to loosely paraphrase Daniel Goleman, it's understanding other people's emotional makeup.

A simple but effective method of boosting one's EQ is an active listening exercise shared by my own leadership coach, based on five steps:

1. Pay attention.
2. Show that you're listening.
3. Provide feedback.
4. Defer judgment.
5. Respond appropriately.

This may sound too simple, or even laughable. Yet just like a strength resistance exercise, the slowest movements are the most challenging. If you find your mind racing ahead in conversation to put your own opinions, thoughts, or suggestions ahead of someone else's, your empathy could use a little work. This exercise requires both restraint and consideration, but the reward is exponential. People who are heard feel respected. And respected people do excellent work.

Seeing Grit in Others

The twenty-first-century job scene is filled with multidimensional candidates and FIT individuals who come with a variety of life experiences. Frequent change between positions isn't always a negative indicator, however; it can indicate an expanded view of the candidate's interests and capacities, as noted by author Claudio Fernández-Aráoz in the book *Great People Decisions*:

> *In this new normal, experience and knowledge are less relevant, while the abilities to learn and adapt, to be resilient and to connect with others, are ever more crucial. Readiness is about the fit between the requirements of the position and the candidate at that particular stage in his or her career. It rests on critical competencies and cultural fit.*

There's that word again: *resilient*. Resilience says more about a person's character than a ten-page résumé. Do they refuse to give up easily? Are they an overcomer? Do they hope for better even with the odds stacked against them? This is the kind of person you want on your team. Dig deep enough in the interview to find out, and you'll know when you've struck gold.

Your Own Grit

You can be sure that the resilience you need is within you, waiting to be utilized. Are there any attitudes or actions or habits in your life that are suppressing that resilience? Identify those now, and deal with them.

Chapter Eight
The Power of Integration

It all began when Sunshine Biscuits put their manufacturing plant on the market. I was young, ambitious, and scaling the corporate ladder in a way that defied conventional notions of a lifelong career at Nabisco. Networking outside the walls of corporate Nabisco in East Hanover, New Jersey, allowed me to create my next career move instead of being led by my circumstances.

Sunshine Biscuits was our number-three competitor in the industry and was selling their facility in Niles, a suburb of Chicago. I informed the senior leadership at Nabisco of the opportunity and provided my rationale for why they should consider buying it. They supported my recommendation and acquired the facility.

Then the senior vice president of manufacturing, who was my internal mentor, suggested I lead this new plant. I was looking for a better FIT in my new job, so I created one where my passion for people could be leveraged. My lack of passion for my old job was draining my energy, so I decided to influence my future with this great company. Early in my professional career, I found the intersection between my skills, the company's needs, and my passion. Some of the best advice to anyone feeling stuck in their job is not to look for something new, but rather to invent it.

Tom McBrady, who reported to the president of Nabisco, was hesitant about my appointment. I was young and without the seniority of a lifer at Nabisco. But my mentor saw a kind of gumption in me that Tom did not. Over time, we arrived at a workable solution.

Nabisco had nine large manufacturing plants at the time, including one that was run by a man named Tony Muscarello. Tony was the plant manager for the Houston facility and was scheduled to retire in a couple of years. He was from the south side of Chicago and formerly worked in Nabisco's largest plant, not far from his father's home. Tony harbored a strong sense of family that reflected something of the mob-boss loyalty that made Chicago famous. His family amassed well over a hundred years of collective service to Nabisco, including his father's forty-year tenure at the Chicago bakery and his uncle's fifty years of service.

Tony was no mob boss, but business meant family to him. This seasoned, industrial-age plant manger moved to Chicago after eighteen years of management at the Houston bakery to become my new boss and mentor. Tony's main objective was to train me in the role of business development manager while overseeing operations and bringing this newly acquired plant into the way of Nabisco.

Forging a New Path

At the time, Nabisco didn't make any products outside its own brand. I helped change that, as Nabisco acquired not only the Niles plant property and equipment but the people who ran its facility. A considerable investment was made in the first year after acquisition to align the plant to Nabisco's brand standards for manufacturing products. I negotiated an agreement between the seller and Nabisco to allow a seamless transition of ownership from Sunshine Biscuits to Nabisco. We made products for Sunshine under the Sunshine and Salerno brands as we readied the plant for Nabisco-branded products. Salerno was famous for its Salerno Butter Cookie radio commercial that ran for three decades and made a comeback in the 1970s.

Tony and I worked well together as the nucleus of a solid FIT team. One of many joint projects was commercializing Nabisco's oatmeal cookies. Commercializing products required standard operating procedures for consistent and reliable quality control. Plant processes and the finished product were tested to ensure consistent production of a high-quality finished product. We ran capability studies which were test runs measuring the true capability of the production process without human interference. If you've ever seen *How It's Made* on the Discovery Channel, you can visualize how this goes. This process resulted in products conveyed through the packaging department without being completely packaged and shipped for distribution into Nabisco's logistics system.

One such test run was underway when I heard shouting at the end of the packaging line between two female employees. The women were visibly upset and yelling in Italian with exaggerated hand gestures and body language. Mr. Salerno was the original owner of the facility, and a loyal Italian community was part of the plant's culture. But I assumed this was a personal conflict and that the women would come to blows. With the help of an area supervisor named Maria, we interpreted the women's concerns. The conflict was of a very different nature than I thought. The women were related to one another, and this communication style was not atypical for how they interacted both at work and in their Italian homes.

The women's conflict was caused by an unexpected clash of cultures in the workplace. Nabisco maintained more rigorous standards in commercializing product than the previous owners had held, and the women's value of frugality was disrupted by Nabisco's capability studies. The female associates thought the study was wasteful and saw no reason for standing by as they watched cookies fall off the end of the conveyor belt without being packaged for sale. In many ways, they were right. There was absolutely nothing wrong with the product; it met all the exacting process and postprocess specifications. But we had to make certain this process was capable, repeatable, and dependable. The female associates were passionate about their job, and would rather package cookies for a consumer than stand by with nothing to do.

Culture Matters

This was a breakthrough learning experience for me. The female associates took pride in their product. They weren't just members of a team, but a family. A process they had championed was transforming before their eyes without an explanation, and they feared losing a unique culture they created. They feared losing their FIT.

Vince Lombardi once said that he loved his Green Bay Packer teammates, but that didn't mean he needed to like them all the time. These women's fierce loyalty to their team meant an initial distrust of Nabisco's new way of doing things when this clash of values occurred. But this was about to change.

Nabisco Niles Bakery FIT team-#1

When Nabisco acquired the Niles Plant, Tony and I met many of the employees, most of them Italian Catholics. This was the second ownership transition many of these tenured associates had experienced with Sunshine.

One morning, they asked us to join them for some kind of ceremony. We found the team gathered in front of the facility, dressed from head to toe in white bakery attire, hair nets, bump caps and all. One woman carried a shovel in her hands. I wondered: Were they bucking the Nabisco way already and burying the new management on the spot? My collar got a little tight as I looked at Tony, who was similarly unaware of what these associates had in mind.

As any good Italian Catholic would do, they had buried a two-foot statue of Saint Joseph, the patron saint of workers, in a flower bed in front of the office for good luck. Catholics appealed to this saint for favor when selling something of personal value. By tradition, the new owners would help them find and exhume the buried saint.

Tony and I spent the next hour digging holes in the front of the plant in search of our good luck. We finally uncovered it, extracted it from the ground, brushed off the dirt, and placed it on a mantel in the main office. Saint Joseph became our FIT mascot. Tony and I laughed a lot that morning; we felt honored that the employees thought to welcome us with this important tradition.

Merging Nabisco with the existing Niles plant culture happened with a little resistance, but it proved successful. Culture is important because it lends the employee a sense of *place* at work. This sense of place ensures people will take ownership of their own success when satisfied with their company's culture. Strong organizational culture fuels a Fully Integrated Team. It takes time, like most other things that are rewarding.

Culture isn't something a company aspires to be; culture is how it already exists. A new leader who aspires to change this will not succeed without respect for the preexisting culture. Many new leaders don't understand this and fail to gain the trust and respect of their team.

Choose wisely when you decide who you want to invite into your FIT house, and recognize early when a relationship simply won't FIT.

Nabisco Takes Notice

When I assumed the plant manager role after Tony's retirement, our FIT team set records for facility and quality audits. People throughout Nabisco took notice. We increased bakery volume exponentially and diversified our portfolio of product lines. Sal Centineo, an area mechanic at the time, expressed his appreciation for this culture of excellence: "We're very proud and thankful to be a part of Nabisco. With all these products, there's a new challenge every day. All the lines are interesting, but fine-tuning the new line of mint SnackWell's is really exciting. I've been here thirty-eight years, and I wish Nabisco had been here from the beginning."

We had created a great FIT.

As our team consistently delivered against expectations, I seldom received calls from headquarters. When I did speak with them, it was assumed I must be spending a fortune to keep the plant running in such great shape. These industrial-age executives at Nabisco adhered to the old carrot-and-stick ideology of management—money was the only driver for a hard-working team. They were wrong. I leveraged a FIT team that was both passionately and intrinsically motivated to do the harder right thing before the easier wrong thing. They took pride in their jobs, in their product, and in each other.

The Niles plant also had the lowest expenses of all of Nabisco plants in maintaining high quality and sanitation. Why? The best quality control system is a FIT team who cares. We used a culture of trust, love, and hard work to reach the plant's desired state with as little waste as possible. We operated like a well-oiled machine—the hallmark of a true FIT.

Team engagement in the workplace is more than a bunch of people working to collect a paycheck every month. The difference when people care is a difference that filters from the work atmosphere right down to product quality. This realization only recently came to the forefront in what Daniel Pink terms the "Conceptual Age." Twenty-first-century workers want much more than a nine-to-five job and a paycheck; they seek an outlet for creativity and empathy.

A Gallup poll conducted in late 2011 report that 71 percent of American workers are "not engaged" or are "actively disengaged" in their work—meaning they're "emotionally disconnected from their workplaces and are less likely to be productive." Emotional disconnect is a rift—a void or lack of understanding between what one feels and what one demonstrates in any relationship, working or otherwise.

This Gallup survey is a reminder of the importance of each individual seeking more than monetary compensation in his work. In the workplace, disengagement most always stems from dysfunction of the individual in a team setting. Important strengths are not being called upon from that person—or, worse yet, they're being ignored. The result is much like a broken limb hanging idly by the body. An emotionally disconnected employee is little more than dead weight.

Leaders may understand this problem best in terms of profit loss and decreased worker productivity. It often must reach this point before someone starts paying attention. In his book *Drive: The Surprising Truth about What Motivates Us,* Daniel Pink reports that disengagement by the American workforce is costing "about $300 billion a year in lost productivity—a sum larger than the GDP of Portugal, Singapore, or Israel." The problem is worsened if the solution is drawn from outdated management styles, as lamented by author Gary Hamel in *The Future of Management:* "Most of the essential tools and techniques of modern management were invented by individuals born in the nineteenth century, not long after the end of the American Civil War."

Management overhaul is desperately needed in our companies and organizations. The workplace once was dominated by a management myth that good performance from employees required strict oversight, along with the old carrot-and-stick rewards-based system. This is increasingly proving to be a myth. What the American worker really needs is a space to exercise his passion and to master a skill set.

Disengagement Creates Risk

I was with a large foods company when I learned for myself what low engagement costs a company, particularly management. In one of the many manufacturing plants I managed, there was an hourly associate whose role was to clean up scrap dough from the production of frozen foods. It turns out the woman had an artistic inclination and shaped figures from the scrap dough to pass to her coworker employed on the opposite end of the fryer line.

It seemed a harmless form of entertainment until one of the woman's dough figurines slipped by her friend onto the fryer line. Her creation was a baby foot sculpture made of dough that was fried, boxed, and packaged for the consumer. When the fated consumer opened up her product, the result was offensive and shocking. The consumer thought it was a real baby foot and called the police! The FBI even got involved, until it was determined that it was only a fried dough sculpture.

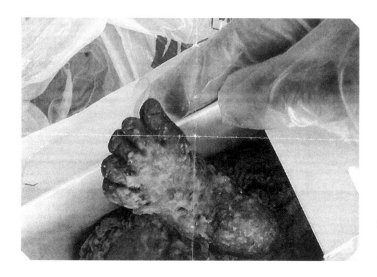

Baby foot sculpture

The employee's disengagement in her role was due to a lack of interest. Her work was better suited for a college art class than a company conveyor belt. People need to feel a holistic connection between who they are and what they do. They need to feel needed, especially in their workplace.

Restructuring workplaces where these kinds of talents can be encouraged and even sponsored by employers is what Matthew Kelly's *The Dream Manager* emphasizes. Kelly asserts that there's a connection between people's daily lives and their dreams. Bridging the gap between the two is how the employer adds value to the life of his or her employee. The "unspoken contract" is how the company values the individual.

Kelly's message is consistent with what my father taught me. Watching him build relationships with people demonstrated the truth of what Henry Ford said: "The secret of success is to understand the point of view of others." It takes constant work to develop this skill set.

The time came for my transition from Nabisco into a new company. I'm much more of a builder than a maintainer, and I become easily bored with the status quo. I left my legacy at the Niles plant in the form of sustainability. It has remained my goal to work myself out of a job, and I've done it more than a few times over my career. Leaders who are successful in building Fully Integrated Teams will stage the organization for success well beyond their departure. I wanted to experience more, and I'd reached my potential at Nabisco from a career-development perspective. Though I loved leading the Niles team and creating a culture of respect for the individual like my father did, it was time for a new challenge.

When I expressed my intent to resign to my boss, he tried to convince me to stay. But after listening to my ambitions, he did what few managers would and supported my decision. My time had come, and my Fully Integrated Team supported my transition forward. It wasn't easy, but it was necessary.

Shifting Gears

A move to Boulder, Colorado, was my family's next adventure, as I took a position as senior vice president of operations at Celestial Seasonings. The incumbent in my position, though classically trained at Frito-Lay and highly competent in operations, was culturally insensitive to Celestial Seasonings as a company. He didn't have the advantage of learning the power of FIT. To add value quickly and make his mark, he imposed the values of Frito-Lay without regard for the employees' preexisting sense of place. He wasn't integrating; he was dominating with a focus on the future and a total disregard of the past. Soon the unions came knocking at his door. The troops were revolting, and the board, including founder Mo Siegal, intervened and let him go. This often happens with companies seeking fast change without understanding their employees' cultural values and needs.

The board at Celestial Seasonings was in search of someone who was a professional supply chain and operations practitioner, and at the end of their six-month search they recruited me. It was a great experience and a lot of fun. We had a Fully Integrated Team for a short period of time, and it created value for all stakeholders.

When the founder and chairman of the board decided to sell the company, it was bad news for the team dynamic. Celestial had been sold once before to Kraft, then resold to its original owner for much less. I guess neither the Frito-Lay way nor the Kraft way were a compatible or an acceptable cultural FIT with the Celestial way. What I learned at the Niles plant would serve me well in this new role.

Celestial Seasonings was sold to the Hain Food Group, and our Fully Integrated Team dissolved. Due to the change of control agreements, many executives cashed out and became very wealthy. Everyone on the senior leadership team left except for me. I was asked to stay by Hain's CEO, Irwin Simon. I agreed, under the conditions that I not cash in all of my fully vested equity awards. I did take some money off the table, but nowhere near as much as I could have. Irwin was very generous in providing me with additional equity awards and opportunities to compensate.

Culture trumps strategy, every time. Eventually, I saw that the cultural differences between the seller and the acquirer of Hain-Celestial were irreconcilable. After maintaining my passion for the job and adding a lot of value to the team and stakeholders, I realized Hain-Celestial was no longer my FIT anymore. I had the utmost respect for Irwin Simon, but I decided to resign. I wasn't willing to mold myself into the organization anymore.

My team and I were together at an off-site meeting when I delivered the news. They were stunned. For cultural reasons alone, I left millions of dollars on the table when I left that organization. I still know it was the right decision. My *purpose* and *principles* were not aligned with theirs; like oil and water, they simply didn't mix. My decision took courage and risk, but I never doubted it was the right one.

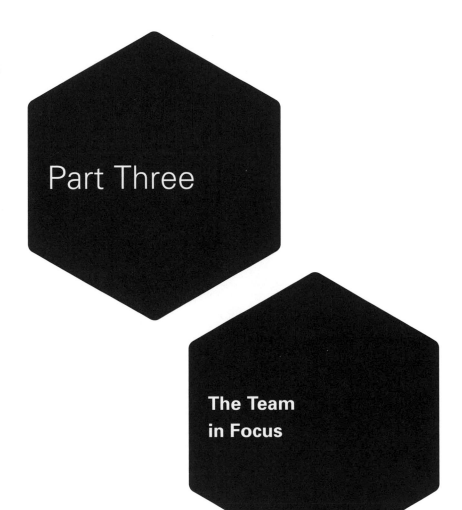

Part Three

The Team
in Focus

Chapter Nine
You and Your Team

In *The Five Dysfunctions of a Team*, Patrick Lencioni teaches us that a lack of trust is the first dysfunction, which in turn leads to further dysfunctions of teams. Throughout my career I've seen this play out in so many ways.

I was once a member of a board of directors comprised of business executives who were seasoned and highly successful. After two years of being a part of this high-powered team, I noticed the culture was far from being nutrient-rich as required in FIT. It had become toxic. None of us looked forward to board meetings. Elephants were always in the room and were mostly avoided at all costs.

In time I felt compelled to discuss this with the board's chairman, who was also the company's CEO. I simply suggested to him that he needed to address this issue. The board had become divided, one side had lost trust in the other, and the CEO and his management team were caught in the middle. Shortly after our brief conversation, the board was reconstituted. Since then, the company's stock has more than tripled. The company has made numerous strategic acquisitions, and everything has sped up.

Without a Fully Integrated Team coming together for a common purpose—with aligned principles and a high level of trust and respect for one another—everything slows down, and in some cases falls apart.

Trust Is the Trump Card

My decision to join Perdue nearly six years ago is marked by a conversation I had with chairman Jim Perdue. My respect for Perdue grew exponentially from my first interactions with him. Jim is a man of his word, and what I expected from him at the outset is what I continue to get. I had plenty of corporate management experience but little know-how in the poultry industry. Jim knew my strengths and weaknesses and saw a transparency in me he trusted.

My battle scars were out in the open—my close encounters with failure that had left a few marks—just as Santiago's hands must have remained deeply scarred from the day he fought to keep his trophy catch. He wore the grit on his hands, and I'm sure those marks triggered more than a question or two.

Jim and I agreed that good leadership at Perdue meant serving well in three areas:

1. Our people

2. Our products

3. Our profitability goals

People first. When you take care of your people, they take care of you. When the time was right, Jim ensured ample opportunity for upward growth in his business. We had a social contract built on trust, an arrangement I wouldn't dream of turning down. I trusted my teammate in a successful career path by which I steadily gained multiple promotions to attain my current position as president of Perdue's foods business, with revenue of 3.5 billion dollars. Jim provided me the opportunity to increase my sphere of influence and lead FIT within his organization. We found the intersection of skills, passion, and needs on a two-way street between employer and employee that was centered in a nutrient-rich place.

Team Building

In my more than thirty-five years of team-building and management, one experience is particularly fresh in memory. It was my second day of work at a new company when I was invited to a senior leadership meeting. The focus was on strategy and financial results, and I decided to learn by observation. In attendance was the chairman, the president of an operations group, the chief financial officer, plus accounting and finance leaders.

I was acquainted with most of the attendees through the interview process. Each gave lip service to the value of teamwork and positivity in their workplace, yet the tension in the board room was palpable, even with the newest member looking on. Short comments and cautious glances glossed over the real issue: a lack of trust. We had a misfit team on our hands.

When the meeting was over, I walked into the president's office and asked: "What was that all about?" He wasn't surprised that I noticed the conflict, and he faulted the CFO. I then went into the CFO's office and asked her the same question. Not surprisingly, she faulted him. Without hesitation, I entered the CEO's office and shared the score of this "he said, she said" game. The look in his eye told me that he knew. The CEO shook his head patiently and admitted that he was working hard to create a high-performance team, but he had a ways to go.

For all companies and teams, sincere beliefs are not enough. FIT directs actions toward alignment of the purpose and principles of the organization. Somehow the leadership overlooked FIT. This team was far from being fully integrated in support of the company's vision, its values, and its reason for being.

Many years after that first dysfunctional meeting, I was offered a promotion. I found myself in the office of the CEO before accepting the offer. I asked, "What will be different?"

He answered in one word: "Trust." He continued, "I trust you to do the right things, the right way, for the right reasons. Everything we do here is built on trust."

This promotion came with a challenge. The organization was not aligned at the top as I'd experienced. Alliances were stranded between leaders within the organization. As a result, everything slowed and in many cases stopped. Little profitable growth occurred within this time period, and the financial results showed it. Despite off-site team-building meetings facilitated by organizational development professionals, the team remained misaligned. The dysfunction trickled into the marketing department (among others), who prepared separate PowerPoint presentations to suit whichever senior team leader was present. This was not a team that trusted.

Without slipping through the necessary filters of my FIT model, the senior leadership team stood to fail. Many people and organizations will face the dilemma of an organization led by a collaborative leader whose business unit manager resists moving the team toward a cohesive vision. The divisive leader then causes factions within the team structure.

Today, that organization is much more FIT than it was so many years ago.

Trust is a feeling authenticated though actions and body language. It was the missing link I sensed in that executive meeting many years ago, and that I labored hard to rebuild over time. "Trust," Stephen Covey says, "is the root of all leadership influence." It's the ingredient FIT teams can't afford to lose. Team alignment with stated company values is what FIT aims to achieve for you and your organization.

The FIT Test

The need for a FIT test emerges here. Take the test below to determine your team or organization's level of FIT, and reap the benefits of expediency in reaching your team's goals.

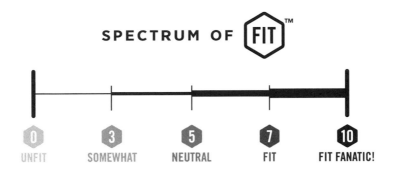

Spectrum of FIT

Answer the following questions with a numbered response indicating FITness, according to the following scale:

0 = not at all (unFIT)

3 = somewhat

5 = neutral

7 = FIT

10 = FIT Fanatic!

Here are the questions:

1. How aligned are you with the organization's *purpose* (reason for being)?

2. How aligned are you with the organization's *principles* (stated values)?

3. How would you rate your team's alignment with the organization's *purpose*?

4.   How would you rate your team leader's alignment with the organization's *purpose*?

5.   How happy are your customers with how you deliver on your *promise*?

6.   To what degree do you feel you have a clear sense of *place* at work?

7.   To what degree does your organization emphasize, embrace, and measure trust?

8.   To what degree does your organization fulfill stakeholders' needs?

9.   To what degree does your organization enhance your skill set?

10.   To what degree is your organization passionate about your personal and professional success?

Add up your answers, then divide the sum by 10 to obtain your FIT test score.

Finding a Better Personal FIT

There are many reasons for finding a new FIT team, and some are inherently positive. Finding a better FIT may mean turning down a *good* opportunity for the *best* opportunity. Such a decision is often not popular or understood by others, but to individuals with grit, the transition makes perfect sense. A singular focus on reaching your goals means closing the door on jobs or situations that detract from the ultimate prize, which is realizing your purpose.

Phil Kassel was a man whose life and FIT journey I invested in. Phil formerly was a regional continuous improvement manager at Perdue. As a solid man and leader, he was dedicated not just to his work but to people first. Shortly after my arrival at Perdue, I met Phil in the process of commissioning a Fully Integrated Team to streamline best practices for continuous improvement at Perdue. This team developed and created the Perdue Business Improvement Process and ensured sustainability for eight plants. Phil was responsible for some of these plants.

In the four years Phil was with Perdue, he and I became friends. He taught me that companies have legacies too, and that the hallmark of any good company is selfless investments.

While Phil had a comfortable job at Perdue, he knew his sense of purpose was not optimally engaged, as was the case in his leadership role at a church community. There he found his passion ignited in a new and thrilling way. Leaving Perdue would require sacrifice, but Phil knew it was the right thing to do. He believed in his new calling as a pastor and speaker.

Having found, now living and preaching, the benefits of FIT

Phil's job transition required him to sell many of his nonessential possessions and accept a pay cut of more than 70 percent. This was a counterintuitive move for most people, but not for Phil. "It required me to give up my title and career path, and to walk away from my pursuit of the American dream," he said. "However, it allowed me to embrace and begin to experience the real dream: life, leadership, and people."

Phil is now the family pastor at a church in Tennessee, where he empowers parents and volunteers to effectively serve in ministry. Just as I helped him find his FIT at Perdue, he now helps ensure FIT in his church community.

Helping people find their needs, skills, and passions in the context of work is a rewarding leadership practice. Leadership is about helping people realize their real dreams. Though Perdue lost a valuable, passionate, talented resource and friend, I supported his decision to follow his purpose.

Some will come to a company or organization and find their ultimate FIT, while others will leave in pursuit of it. This is the ebb and flow of FIT individuals taking hold of their dreams.

Profiling Your FIT Team

Individuals like Phil are acutely aware of when to stay and leave, while others may not be so adept in assessing their best fit with a particular company. A responsible leader assesses who is supporting a team's growth as well as who is polluting it. Despite the goodwill that most people possess, there are a few who turn problematic when their lack of passion for the job or their refusal to cooperate creates an unFIT dynamic.

The Ropella Group, a globally renowned executive search and talent management firm, uses three terms to classify supportive and destructive roles within a team:

- *Loyalists:* They consistently spot problems but also create solutions.
- *Benign saboteurs:* They have little or no concern for the interests of the company; they may even observe acts of terrorism and ignore them as if nothing ever happened.
- *Terrorists:* They consistently create problems and confrontations to spawn conflict and derision.

In this context, "terrorism" describes acts within the team that are a deliberate, planned threat to the team's ultimate success. Terrorists are not aligned with the fundamental purpose; in fact they're vehemently set against it. Like it or not, your team may have a terrorist or two, or even a benign saboteur whose lack of effort is wreaking damage similar to that caused by the schemes implanted by terrorists.

Watch for the kind of personas and calculated conflicts that result only in distraction or strife between team members.

Creating a Fully Integrated Team is hard work, and knowing who is not aligned with your organization is an important step. A team member who's regularly inciting conflict and flare-ups must be removed. They'll damage both the morale of your team and the growth of your organization in a hurry.

Restructuring Your FIT Team

I once inherited a team that included two people who proved incapable of collaboration as they undermined the efforts and culture we were trying to create. To respect their privacy, we'll call them Kate and John.

Many of the meetings Kate and John attended resulted in highly charged emotional situations. I started bringing tissues to our meetings in preparation for the fallout. In time, however, I realized that this would not work. Our team's trust was fractured, and progress was suffering. Kate and John weren't going to exchange their old habitual feelings against one another. When I learned that one of them had stepped outside the boundaries of the company's stated cultural values, I addressed the issue outright.

I confronted Kate and John both individually and together. Though initially things seemed to be improving, I could feel the distrust and hate growing between them. I called one last meeting with them to address the breach of values within the company, and I explained why this behavior was unacceptable. After gaining confirmation that company values had been violated, I asked both to wait while I went to see the CEO.

I was looking for his support, to test the principles of our organization at its highest level. I was hoping to find them steadfast. Entering his office, I addressed him point-blank with this question: "If someone doesn't align with our values and consistently steps outside the boundaries of those values, would you support my decision to let this person go?"

There was hardly a pause before he agreed.

What followed is never the highlight of anyone's career. I let a team member go—because it was the right thing to do. I helped him find a better FIT elsewhere and removed the toxic environment his loyalist team member Kate was living in and replaced it with a nutrient-rich environment where she could thrive.

Letting Your Team Teach You

Intentionality is a best practice for relationships. Those we surround ourselves with determine the kind of people we are.

One intentional relationship that shapes me is with my life coach. I get a kick-start to my week in my biweekly conversations with Greg. We discuss areas of improvement and things or projects I'm passionate about, and he responds with insights on how to improve my performance as a FIT individual and leader. The four dimensions we cover are *spiritual, emotional, intellectual,* and *physical.* I keep a scorecard to track progress in each area, reviewing it with Greg. He provides me with fresh energy and inspiration. Greg is one of many members of my Fully Integrated Team.

No man is an island unto himself. Those given to negative thoughts must seek relationships as an escape from their own mental prisons. If there's no one to speak positivity into negative beliefs, they turn destructive.

Thoughts, choices, and actions are all behaviors that move us along a continuum between unsuccessful living and a life filled with joy and happiness. Thoughts come from environment. That's why the proper environment is so crucial to well-being.

External feedback from a mentor is imperative to success because sometimes we're blinded by our own weaknesses. That's why it's rare to see professional athletes without coaches. A golfer may have a swing coach, a short-game coach, a fitness trainer, and a sports psychologist on his team. These top performers know the value of solid, constructive feedback from experts. They understand what they need to reach the summit of their profession—right thinking, hard work, a nurturing environment, and timely and actionable feedback. Successful people have Fully Integrated Teams.

This kind of partnership provides accountability for reaching your goals. If no one is there to cheer you on in adhering to a new fitness plan, or to sign up for that competitive sales contest at work, or to take the lead on a company project, how can you be expected to think or achieve differently?

We need the help of others to step outside our comfort zones into an environment where more learning and improvement can occur. I've learned in many years of teamwork that I cannot shoulder full responsibility for failure or success alone. It's that smoke-and-mirrors principle my father iterated to me again and again: *things get done with people.*

People need people, and partnership always requires time and humility. It's not always easy to see another person's perspective, but it's certainly more healthy than being fed one's own ideas and thoughts all the time. When others expect great things from us, we rise to the occasion. It takes a conscious effort to transform the world of our thought life, but FIT enacts both order and structure to make it a little less like a Wild West show, where anything goes. Success is the fruit of grit, not an immediate outcome.

Riding with Carl

How you see the world is critical and impacts your thinking and behavior. Therefore, one of the characteristics that FIT leaders develop is the ability to see the world through the lens of other people, team members and other stakeholders.

Everything at Perdue starts with people. Once a year the company sponsors Driver Appreciation Week. It provides management with the opportunity to ride with one of our company drivers to learn more of what they do, and to thank them for it.

Once I had the opportunity to ride with Carl. I met Carl at our Salisbury, Maryland feed mill where we picked up a load of feed for chickens to be delivered to a chicken farm about an hour away. Carl has been driving for Perdue for thirty-three years.

I jumped in his rig and buckled my seat belt. Off we went, two strangers working for the same company in two very different roles, and two people who live their lives in very different environments. I'm a fifty-six-year-old and Carl is a fifty-seven-year-old. That's pretty much where the similarities ended.

After engaging in active listening and getting to know each other, Carl asked me if I had family. I shared with him about my wife, Fritzi, and our two grown children. I mentioned how our daughter, Lauren, is a second-year teacher at a high school teaching Advanced Placement Psychology as well as other related classes. And I told how our son, Jimmy, is a senior at the University of Wisconsin, preparing to take his law school admittance test, with hopes for open doors at competitive law schools.

Then I asked Carl about his family. He told me had seven kids and twenty-five grandchildren. None of his kids were married, and one of his sons is in jail for selling drugs. He spoke of his family and his situation in the same proud tone I spoke of mine. Carl visits his son in jail, and hopes he finds a better FIT went he gets out in another few years.

What hit me is how different our lives are. When he leaves work for the day, he leaves his work behind. I take mine with me, 24-7.

Seeing the Word through Others' Eyes

My father and his friend George Markham began traveling to Central America to fish in the 1960s. I was grateful to have been provided an open invitation to join them and other friends on their annual winter trip. Fortunately I was able to do so a dozen or so times.

One year we went to Costa Rica, to the remote village of Parismina. Within this village was a small fishing camp. The captains of the boats were natives to the village.

One day when were out on the water fishing, our boat's captain took us to an island where natives lived. As we came in close to this small village, we saw a small wood thatch-roofed hut with smoke coming out of a chimney. A child and his mother came out the front door. I soon realized this was the captain's wife and daughter awaiting his arrival.

And I was about to discover they were also waiting for what would be served as dinner.

On our boat, the captain reached down into a cubby and pulled out a live five-foot iguana. The iguana's toenails were pulled so that the tendons were exposed and used to tie its legs behind its back.

The captain threw out an anchor into waist-deep water, grabbed the iguana, threw it over his shoulder, jumped into the water, and waded to shore to meet his family. After hugs and kisses he handed his wife the live iguana, which would (I assumed) be the center-of-the-plate protein for dinner.

As this was happening, dugout canoes filled with young children were heading toward us from the village. The villagers were standing on the beach watching all of this. You couldn't help noticing the smiles on their face.

That's when my father leaned over to me and said, "Jim, I am so glad we were able to see this together. I'm not certain what we are seeing will still be here someday down the road. Look how happy these people are. I hope we don't send our people down here to mess all this up."

The lesson here for me was about how I see the world. How these natives of Costa Rica viewed their world was much different than how the people on our block back at home see it. I learned the valuable lesson of the value of simplicity that day. These natives were living very happy, simple lives, and it showed in the smiles on their faces.

Chapter Ten
Living and Leading FIT

Leaders will be asked to make value judgments in the workplace. It's often thought we'll meet these decision points in a grand confrontation with selfishness or temptation, when in fact it's all about the little decisions we make along the way.

My father taught me to deal fairly with others not just in words, but also through relationships and actions. My father's example would come in handy when I received an unexpected phone call from Corporate Nabisco.

Letting Principles Guide Your Decisions

I was still under the leadership of Tony at the time and was chomping at the bit to take the reins of the Niles plant upon his retirement. Tony's office and mine were set up right next to each other. The administrative assistant we shared came into my office and said that the senior vice president of manufacturing was on the phone. He was my mentor and Tony's boss, the same person who supported my transition to leadership at the Niles facility.

The conversation quickly turned from pleasantries to the business at hand. He called to inform me that a corporate jet was scheduled to pick Tony up and fly him to corporate headquarters in New Jersey where he would be asked to resign as plant manager of the Niles facility. I was selected to succeed him as plant manager as soon as they delivered the news.

Something about the conversation moved me at a gut level. I knew that what was happening to Tony wasn't right, so I asked why corporate was removing him. His response was stern: "We have reviewed allegations that Tony knowingly shipped product that did not meet Nabisco standards." I assured him that I must be responsible somehow for the violation of product standards along with our Fully Integrated Team. He replied that I wasn't implicated in the complaint, and he gave strict instructions to keep our conversation private before he ended the call.

I sat at my desk, dizzied by the weight of our conversation but knowing what I had to do. I walked into Tony's office, discreetly closed the door behind me and told him everything. He was just as shocked as I was. I walked back into my office to call my mentor back, offering the same respect I gave Tony: full disclosure. There was more than a brief pause on the other end of the phone when I told him what I'd done. "You did what?" he choked in disbelief. "Don't you want to run that plant? My God, you'll be plant manger tomorrow!"

My response carried a firm tone: "Of course I do, but I will not work for any company that treats its people the way you've asked me to treat Tony. He's a guy I've come to respect, who has gone out of his way for this company over his long career, and he would never do what you're alleging." I was sure I'd just blown any future promotion with Nabisco, and maybe even for the rest of my career.

I waited to hear the dial tone; instead, my mentor replied, "This is exactly why you're the right guy for the job, Jim. From our visits, it's clear why the people there love and respect you. Tony will still come here, and we'll decide upon his exit date. I'll let you know when that transition occurs." With that, he hung up the phone. The allegation against Tony turned up false, and he retired from the company of his own accord.

I can't imagine making any other decision than the one I made that day. It defied the course of action that Nabisco pressured me to take, but my personal values held firm. I couldn't support Nabisco ousting a man without a fair hearing, a man whose family had given more than a hundred years of service to Nabisco. Despite the bait of a good promotion, something wasn't right, and I knew it.

The power behind a FIT team is loyalty, and it's certainly a force to be reckoned with.

My intrinsic value of serving and respecting people helped me to make the right decision when it mattered most. I knew what a promotion with the largest cookie and cracker company in the world could do for my career. I could have let corporate handle my transition into leadership as they saw fit. But in light of the false allegations against Tony, I would have regretted it immensely.

Had I made the decision not to intervene in Tony's forced resignation, I would have been playing the role of Benign Saboteur within my Fully Integrated Team—watching passively as a great mentor and an asset to our success became an afterthought. This wouldn't do. I couldn't let that happen, and my decision to act as a loyalist—even at the risk of losing corporate trust—was worth taking a stand. I gained respect that day, both from Tony and from corporate, which I carried into promotions that didn't require a compromise of my personal values.

Many of us will face decisions like this—moments when making the right decision matters most. We're all faced with opportunities to wound or inspire others, and the results will have rippling effects.

It has served me well to view leadership not as a one-time decision, but as a legacy to be inherited by my children. FIT leaders always act for the benefit of others, just like my father did. As Phil Kassel says, "Leadership is not about self-indulgence, but rather selfless investments."

The power of leadership, when handled correctly, achieves every leader's dream: a team that trusts.

Living FIT by Applying Grit

The vision was a sprint triathlon in late June—something to commit all my air to, something big. At fifty-six, the responsibility of a four-billion-dollar business wasn't enough. More than a challenge, I wanted to compete again.

I had successfully completed a few Olympic distance triathlons in my twenties while living in California. I was familiar with the physical rigor involved: runs in the dark at four A.M., riding my bike on the weekends and after work, drives to and from the pool. Triathlon training was routine, and most days looked and felt the same: hard. But the vision of finishing in the top three of my age group pulled the grit out of me.

Jim and Lauren

On race day, my daughter Lauren and I woke at five A.M. and headed for the beach. She was standing in for my wife and son who were traveling for his upcoming internship as a staffer for a state senator in Wisconsin. After staging my bike and gear in the transition zone, Lauren and I walked down the beach to view a sunrise over the Atlantic, something I've seen hundreds of times but which still captivates me. The night before, I had visualized the swim, the road, and my heart beating all the way to the finish line. I pictured the Post-it on my desk at work with my goal times. In my mind's eye, I saw Lauren cheering her "pops" on to the victory of a top three finisher, exhausted but feeling great.

The race began in waves to space out the competitors. I was in the third wave, surrounded by red swim caps. As we clumped together at the starting line, my body surged with anticipation. I couldn't wait to get into the water; I always felt comfortable in it.

At the crack of the gun signal, we scattered into the surf. The first leg of the race was a half mile of open ocean, fairly calm with bit of high surf. Five minutes in, my muscles felt tense and exhausted. The surf made it difficult to see the other competitors. Allowing my muscle memory to crowd out fatigue, I turned north around the first big buoy, thinking, *Relax, pull hard and swim straight, just like in practice.*

As I rounded the final buoy, I drove hard toward the shoreline with the tide's pull advancing and receding like a washing machine.

When my feet hit the sand, I came up out of the shallows and into the transition zone to the sound of Lauren's voice: "Go, Pops! Only two young guys ahead in your wave." She knew my vision and was the perfect person to spur me on. This was a bigger goal than I could achieve alone.

Leading the Pack

Stripping free of my wet suit layers, my skin hit the fresh ocean air. The next leg was a bike race. With the help of my biking coach Steve, I'd learned to use Aero bars on my new Cervélo bike, keeping my body aerodynamic and sleek. The challenge was maintaining that position without straining the bad disc in my lower back. Just three months prior, I had injured my back while training and had undergone physical therapy. Dr. Horsey helped strengthen my core muscles and the hamstring and tendons on my right leg I had detached from my pelvis in a waterskiing injury two years earlier. With the limited flexibility of my right leg on the first day of therapy, he was amazed I was able to run at all. Since then, I'd come a long way with his help.

I relaxed into the music of my pedal strokes and was surprised to see my speed averaging above my personal best. All those hours in the saddle were paying dividends. Each competitor wore their age across the back of the lower leg, and I was careful not to let anyone slip by in my age bracket. I even enjoyed passing some of those who were less than half my age.

I came into the next transition zone and spotted Lauren there, cheering me on. She uplifted my spirits even as back spasms plagued me. *Just relax*, I pleaded with my body, determined not to give in. As I found my stride, the spasms subsided enough for me to finish the race. Gritting out the finishing stretch, I propelled what was left of me across the finish line with no regrets. Based on my overall time, I knew I'd raced my best. I left nothing on the course but sheer exhaustion and a tremendous sense of accomplishment. And the results were in: I'd won in my age group!

Jim postrace

Lauren immediately called Fritzi and Jimmy to share the news. My wife's tearful response affirmed it was a mutual victory. She knew how hard I'd trained for this. The only thing sweeter than success was sharing it with my Fully Integrated Team—my wife and kids, my triathlon coach Steve, my physical therapist Richard, and my executive coach Greg. I also knew my dad was with me in spirit; I envisioned that familiar twinkle in his eye and knew I'd taken his advice to heart in creating a Fully Integrated Team to help me reach a collective win. Without that team's skills and passions, victory wasn't possible.

Well-being is far more than physical exercise; it's also peace of mind. As president of Perdue Foods, helping others get one step closer to FIT means being the first to practice it. I want people to expect that I have their best interests in mind. It's my most important job. Alongside our chairman and "head cheerleader," Jim Perdue, I'm the front-runner to advance people's trust and well-being as the core of our company. Simon Sinek expresses it this way:

> *The leader sitting at the top of the organization is the inspiration, the symbol of the reason we do what we do. They represent the emotional limbic brain. WHAT the company says and does represents the rational thought and language of the neocortex.*[1]

Leading a FIT Culture

The leader sets the tone for a healthy culture by empowering people to pursue a common purpose in alignment with the company's principles. Of course, the best way to do this is by modeling health for your FIT culture. I start my day in one of two ways: either a six-mile run or an eighteen-mile bike ride. At the four-mile mark of my morning run, I stop at the end of South Point. The view is spectacular overlooking Sinepuxent Bay, Assateague Island, and the Atlantic Ocean. I time my run to hit the four-mile mark as the sun rises over the barrier island. There I give thanks to God for my many blessings and ask for support in my service to others.

My early morning runs prepare me physically and emotionally for work each morning. It requires a fair amount of grit on days I don't feel so well, but in the end, I'm always refreshed by this morning ritual. A "have-to" approach to exercise would quickly diminish my sense of refreshment and discipline. The same is true for work. A good leader knows that part of empowering others to do the right thing is to care for their personal health. Each human being was made for greatness, but must be equipped.

At Perdue, we have something called the Perdue Health Improvement Program (HIP) pioneered by Dr. Roger Merrill, our chief medical officer and Jim Perdue, our Chairman. This progressive and competitive offering for associates in the poultry and agribusiness industry began in 2004 and remains a priority at Perdue.

Each year, twenty thousand Perdue associates are presented the option of HIP participation, including a voluntary health questionnaire regarding habits, biometric measurements of blood pressure, weight, and body fat percentage, along with blood tests for cholesterol, tobacco, and diabetes indicators. Individual data is then collected to assess the most dangerous preventable disorders in that individual. HIP also provides health coaches for at-risk associates to help them move toward a healthier desired future state.

HIP boasts almost 90 percent participation company-wide, without providing employees financial incentive for their participation. This is substantially higher than the average participation rate (40 percent) in similar programs at other companies. One of every five Perdue associates has dramatically improved their health as a result of HIP with lower blood pressure or cholesterol, weight loss, or kicking a tobacco habit, alongside many more who've realized improved health through the discovery of treatable cancers and adherence to new exercise programs.

Wellness centers opened their doors alongside even the most remote plant locations to provide hourly associates and their dependents better access to primary care, including women's preventative services and treatment of diabetes, asthma, and flu. The proof is in the pudding as far as Dr. Merrill is concerned, who describes our wellness centers as "an immediate and measurable success; medical inflation was tamed, health improved, and associate satisfaction rose."

When companies like Perdue show they care by providing a unique service, a new standard forms in the industry that competitors must respond to. This creates value for associates, for their dependents, and for the communities where Perdue is located. It's virtually inevitable that when Perdue's people are taken care of, profitability ensues.

With this successful program intact, I've challenged Dr. Merrill and his staff to expand this program to include a happiness program and score. Now that we've assessed how physically healthy our associates are, the program ventures to measure the quality of life of each person at Perdue. Dr. Merrill and his staff did an informal survey of associates in Perdue plants to find out what made them happy. Not even those who struggled to meet their family's basic needs on an hourly income responded with "Money."

Many reported that HIP was a major workplace satisfier, affirmed by findings that HIP participants are one third as likely to leave the company than their matched non-participants. Participation in HIP was indicating long-term investment in Perdue. Emotional health, physical health, social health, and spiritual health were the responses indicative of employee happiness.

Dr. Merrill's compassion for people is driven by his interest to see others at their healthiest and happiest. Dr. C. Everett Koop, former U.S. surgeon general and personal mentor to Dr. Merrill, has stated that 70 percent of our medical expenditures and personal health problems in the United States are attributable to lifestyle modifiable factors. This means that most of the medical problems Americans endure are highly preventable—yet evidence consistently shows that only 10 percent of those who've had heart bypass surgery or angioplasty make changes to their diet and lifestyle after the procedure. Old habits die hard.

When I transitioned into my role as president at Perdue, I required the management team to review HIP participation and aggregated (not individual) health scores of departments under their direct supervision. I wanted leaders to know the big picture of their people, what kind of struggles their employee population was experiencing, and how they might be able to help. I wanted my managers to put their people first. I know how efficient it is for so many leaders to operate in broad strokes without taking the time to gain detailed knowledge about their team. I was passionate to create a leadership that genuinely cared for Perdue's associates.

The HIP has many successes to boast of, but the foremost is the traction gained with the hourly associates. They've shown greater strides toward improving their health than any other population at Perdue, a trend that initially shocked Dr. Merrill. But in conversation with a twenty-eight-year-old single mom and production foreman, he began to understand. She described the wellness center as "the only place I ever go in life where someone cares about me just because I'm me—not because they can sell me something, or buy something from me, or I can do them some service. Why would anyone ever leave a company like that?"

Chapter Eleven
Bringing Change

Whenever I get a sniff of diesel-filled exhaust, my mind brings me back to the Tropic Star Lodge in Panama. I can see the end of the pier, where eight diesel-powered inboard fishing boats idle patiently. I can also see my father there, standing next to me. Thick black smoke settles over the jungle and the crowd of sixteen anglers, who are eager to get offshore.

This memory is so real, it's as if I'm standing there now. It's a living piece of history my mind formed around like wet cement. I can recall the sights, sounds, and smells with perfect clarity.

Dad and me on one of my first fishing trips to Panama

I guess those images could be called pieces of my father's legacy. These dynamic memories shape the person I am today.

Creating reality begins in our minds. But it doesn't just stay there, moving from thought to action. As the authors of *Full Steam Ahead* suggest, "The images we hold in our minds have a tremendous impact on the realities we create." Those images become part of us.

The profound reality of leadership is that what we do matters. In the words of Brian Tracy, "As a manager, everything you do or say either builds people up or pulls them down. Concerning your behaviors and the emotions of the people who report to you, nothing is neutral." Or as I often say, *everything communicates.*

This means that a life of serving others will never lack influence or purpose. It also means that I'm responsible for creating the negative or positive legacy for those vested in my Fully Integrated Team. Building a legacy with others is a great privilege, but it isn't something that arises haphazardly. We all need to take the time to ask ourselves, Where will I leave my fingerprints? What and who will I touch? What impact will I make in the lives of those I serve? What will my dash be?

In my thirty-five-plus years in leadership and management, I've learned something very important: people don't have to be closed, rigid systems of habits and thoughts that stay on a single track from now until eternity. They can *change*—which means *so can you*. The rate of change external to yourself and your organization should be less than the change happening within your organization. If you're stagnant, you'll lose the race.

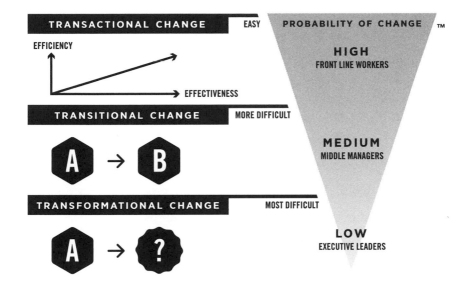

FIT Change Model

When thinking of and coaching people and organizations through change, I use the FIT Change Model. The left side of the model represents three different types of change. The right side of the model represents who is responsible for what kind of change. Transactional change is the easiest and is mostly done by frontline team members. Its focus is getting to a desired result (effectiveness) with as little waste as possible (efficiency). Transitional change requires moving from a current state to a well-defined desired state. Middle management is typically responsible for transitional change. The most difficult category of change is transformational change. This is usually the result of realizing that the current state is no longer acceptable and therefore must be changed, but no one is yet certain of what the future changed state looks like. This is the job of executive leadership.

There are few experiences, even the negative ones, that cannot be used for growth and expansion. Remember to fail small and forward. This is exciting! How deeply meaningful our lives truly are. Whether I'm looking out over the Atlantic during a morning workout or from 30,000 feet in my business travels, I recount many of my life's experiences, feeling as if it's all happened in a blink. It's a rewarding life, and it's one *you* can create.

Once we have a clear vision of our desired state, words like "I wish" and "aspiring" and "someday" belong nowhere near our vocabulary. Aspirations are not physical actions. As leaders of our own legacy, we create, we do not wait. Moving forward in the creation of the rest of your dash, are you a spectator, a dreamer, or a doer? Your legacy is hanging in the balance.

The spectator loves to give his opinion almost as much as an ESPN sports analyst does. His specialty is critique, the easiest job on the planet. Nothing materializes into real, concrete action with a critic. He's unwilling to get onto the field, and he's unFIT to lead.

The dreamer has a lot of thoughts worth listening to. He takes a step further than the spectator in moving toward potential solutions, but he sees in broad strokes, losing track of important details. He's content to imagine instead of execute, to describe instead of show, and he's notoriously bad with deadlines. The dreamer lends constructive ideas but lacks the organization to see them through, until the doer steps in.

The doer is the universal taskmaster, with a list and pen always in hand. He combines the constructive criticism of team members and past experience to inform his future plans. He's structured and he plans the microsteps involved in reaching his goals. His penchant for discipline helps him succeed and complete each step with diligence. He's futuristic but also realistic.

FIT people take action upon their dreams and legacies, like the doer. They create a vivid description of a desired future state like the dreamer, and bring it back to the present, creating a plan to get there. They take disciplined action, hour by hour, day by day, one year at a time. They take roles as both strategist and executor, dreamer and doer.

Unfit people observe and complain from the bleachers, like the spectator, but they refuse to get in the game. A doer gets in the game.

Going from dreaming to doing isn't always easy. It's a change most people desire but fear. If I want to lose ten pounds, my desired state is easy to envision. It's the dozens of hours in the gym and daily sacrifice of tempting foods that require endurance.

Getting Everyone on the Same Page

After meeting with executives about driving better alignment and integration in a large consumer packaged goods company, I began leveraging the FIT model by asking them to articulate for me their need. I was searching for the intersection of their needs, my skills, and how passionate we all were in solving their problems—in other words, creating and sustaining FIT.

After a fairly intense session of active listening, I played back to them what I thought I was hearing. Their need was to "get FIT." Without getting into the details and complexities of their situation, what they were experiencing was a lack of alignment in their organization's processes; they weren't linked or synced. There was no single version of the truth. The various cells of this organization were not working together as a division of labor supporting one common cause. It was a house divided.

We determined that we quickly needed to standardize around best practices and fully aligned and integrated people across the various functions to drive change in what they were doing—and, more importantly, *how* they were doing what they did. As a result of our decision, a work charter is now being created which will include job scope, timelines, deliverables, critical success factors, and names of core and support team members.

In this particular organization's case, it will take a full year to significantly improve their FITness score across the multiple organizational dimensions we agreed upon in the meeting. We'll first define the organization's *purpose* and *principles*. We'll then make certain we have the right people on the bus and in the right seats, people who are as passionate about the organization as the organization needs to be about them. Then we'll develop a strategic plan that will deal with the organization's *promise* and *place,* to be built upon the foundation of purpose, principles, and people.

I share this brief story to give you a feel of how FIT might work in your organization. At some point in the process, the power of FIT comes alive and is very visible. You can see it and feel it when you first walk in a business. There's a high level of energy, enthusiasm, health, and happiness.

As you work through the FIT process, it gains momentum and becomes contagious. People in the organization observe this phenomenon and become curious. It can happen in a manufacturing plant, in corporate headquarters, or within a team.

As I mentioned earlier, my daughter Lauren teaches Advanced Placement Psychology at a local high school in Berlin, Maryland. Lauren recently shared with my wife and me how she and her students conducted a creative experiment that communicated the power of FIT.

After properly advising the high school's administration, Lauren and her students all gathered around during a period between classes when the hallways were bustling with students and looked toward the ceiling in the foyer of the high school.

As hypothesized, more and more students who were not in on the experimental design stopped and looked up as well. Remember, everything communicates, and if you create something remarkable with your FIT, people will take notice and want to join in on the fun.

That's the fun part of FIT...and it takes *grit.*

The Five D's: Debate, Decide, Declare, Deliver, and Discipline

In leading FIT and bringing change, our goals must be approached with structure and preparation—a game plan I call the Five D's.

When a discussion makes a turn toward debate, many people cringe. Cultural politeness is partly to blame for avoiding opinions unlike your own. But different isn't always a bad thing; in fact, it's a sign of health. Debate is the seed of change. FIT organizations debate at a logical versus emotional level. They have high organizational EQ's and don't interpret lively discussion as a personal assault. Healthy FIT teams value and trust the input of their peers; though they might disagree, it helps lead a team toward the right decision. Having trust and respect among FIT members is vital. It's also why starting with a shared and common belief is so important. It's difficult for team members to respect and trust one another if their fundamental beliefs aren't somewhat aligned.

But when it comes to having a team that cannot agree on a solution, it's almost better than having a team that refuses to contribute. Debate indicates which side of the fence your team is on. This reminds me of one lifeless meeting I attended at Nabisco headquarters, so sedentary that the motion-sensored lights turned off in the room! Apathy is an unsuspecting but dangerous vice that will crumble a FIT team more effectively than controversy.

Meetings must generate results. Reaching decisions is a weakness for many teams, especially those whose meetings lack a goal or outcome. Declare intentions publicly. Record and keep them in front of your desk on a Post-it note. Restate your intentions at the beginning of each group meeting to help you refocus. Champion other members when they complete relevant tasks, and commit yourself to getting your own results.

In his book *Piloting Strategy*, my friend John Delany asks, "Now that I have a strategy, what do I do?" Planning without execution is like thought without action. Both may point toward a desired state, but neither will get you there.

Do your work with a winning attitude, grit, and discipline, and people will notice. Coworkers appreciate team members who contribute not begrudgingly but with a sincerity to help others. A hard worker builds a good reputation for himself in finding nothing to complain about. Dare to set yourself apart, and work hard!

Disciplined Strategy Wins

Discipline is never a natural result but a concerted daily effort. Jim Collins terms discipline a "twenty-mile march" of consistent and strategic steps toward the same goal, which he captures with the stories of two exploration teams in the early nineteenth century who raced to be the first to reach the South Pole. Both expedition leaders had comparable qualifications and strengths to face the same unforgivable subzero temperatures and high winds. Each had a seemingly equal shot at winning, yet one team was successful and the other team was not. Why?

As Collins summarizes, the successful expedition members exhibited traits that "reject the idea that forces outside their control or chance events will determine their results; they accept full responsibility for their own fate... then bring this idea to life by a triad of core behaviors: fanatic discipline, empirical creativity, and productive paranoia. And they all led their teams with a surprising method of self-control in an out-of-control world."[1]

Based on fanatic planning, discipline, and grit, one team escaped with a win and their lives while the other perished in failure. It's not your plans that manifest themselves in your FIT legacy; it's your *actions*. So many people err in thinking that it comes easy to some and hard to others. Discipline is easy for no one. It's a war, and it's won or lost on the battleground of daily decisions and actions.

The doer understands this perfectly. Discipline is the stepladder by which he achieves his goals. The sustainable infrastructure of discipline ensures that the process can be repeated to achieve even greater goals and aspirations. The world is full of people who "wanted to" but never did because they were looking for shortcuts.

The Parable of Talent Investment

A notable work ethic is praised even in the Bible as the hallmark of a strong, moral person. The parable of the talents is one account. "Talents" were the monetary currency at the time the story was told, a story that also serves as a lesson to us in modern times in how to invest our own resources.

The businessman in the parable gives each of his three servants a portion of his talents to invest on his behalf while he's away on a trip. After some time, the man returns from his journey and pays a visit to each servant to see what kind of investment was made with the lended money. The first two servants have productive yields on their investments, with double to show for what the man loaned them. He praises their productive efforts, saying, "Well done, good and faithful servant; you were faithful over a few things, I will make you ruler over many things." The reward for their efforts is more responsibility—promotions to a higher level of trust to handle his business affairs.

But the last servant comes up short. He has done nothing with the talent he was loaned. For fear of making the wrong choice, he has shirked his responsibility to do his best and has buried the money in the ground—a way of safekeeping the money before there were banks. The returned businessman is profoundly disappointed at this last servant's lack of initiative; he takes back his investment, and gives it to the others.

The talents in this story represent virtually anything that's valuable to your team or employer. It could be a fresh perspective, an innovative solution, an aptitude, a skill set, or a work ethic. But it means nothing if we withhold our contribution from our team. Many of us don't risk because we're afraid of failure. Yet in many ways, it's the only way to grow. Connecting the dots to your designed future will not be safe. But it will be exceedingly better than the future someone else will plan for you. The fear of failure, despite consenting opinions, is a healthy thing. Remember, Fully Integrated Teams and individuals grow by failing often and forward.

Imagine a dash that says, "Here lies Jim Leighton; he was afraid to fail, lived a safe life, and accomplished little. He lived an unremarkable life."

My point is to get out there and make some noise. Don't quit and stay put; live to make a difference in other people's lives. If a goal or project you've commissioned doesn't scare you and your FIT at times, and doesn't challenge the stuff you're made of, then the goal isn't worth the time and effort. Growth comes from discomfort. If we discipline our fears with preparation and grit, we'll accomplish great things. But this kind of motivator is strictly personal. As a leader and team member, never use fear to motivate others. Fear-driven manipulation will result in work at the expense of the individual and the team. Instead, choose individuals who are self-motivators, those innately driven by a challenge.

Control What You Can

Leaving a legacy begins with the tiny seed of character. Just a struggling shoot at first, it grows in the face of adversity into something majestic, something people see and want to follow.

A small book called *It's Not about You* contains some great pithy suggestions on how to lead well. In it, the author says something poignant: "Economies rise and fall. Circumstances change. We bleed. We heal. We grow. Sometimes we end up in Critical Care. We can't control any of it, not really. What we *can* control is *who we are*"—and, I would add, *who we will become*.

As leaders, we shouldn't feel handicapped by the factors out of our control. But maximizing those we can control and minimizing the negative effects of what we cannot is essential. How we react to trying circumstances defines us. It's the reason people entrust their dreams and futures into our care every day, and it's something that can make or break one's leadership. Even as I write this book, the industry in which my FIT team competes is highly volatile—but we're paving our success in the midst of it.

Frontline Leadership

Having a laugh with FIT members who do the real work

A FIT leader is available, visible, and involved. Whether in the nosebleed section or on the front lines, a leader is ear-up to the pulse of his organization. He sees the ebb and flow of the work process, where the bright stars of leadership are forming, and the points at which initiatives are straying off course or weakening the goal.

I had my first real lesson in FIT leadership while working the front line in the cookie and cracker industry as a young man. After founding National Health Management Company and my time with Matrix One, I called up my dad to seek his career mentorship. Invested in the consumer packaged goods food and beverage industry for most of his life, he connected me with the Ellis family who owned the Indiana franchise for Archway Cookies. They were building a business in South Beloit, Illinois to produce cookies and confections for their fundraising business, the kind students peddle to raise money for their school band or athletics.

When I met with Rob Ellis, one of the owners, I fully expected him to offer me a front office job where I could suit up in tie and shirt to "learn the business." I was wrong. Rob had consulted my father and together they directed me to the shop floor for the first part of my new career in this unfamiliar industry. Rob said I wouldn't be provided the opportunity to work as a manager or supervisor until I learned from the shop floor associates how to operate every piece of equipment in the plant. I was to first earn their respect. Rob challenged me to get to know everyone in the plant by their first names and learn about their families and why they came to work every day. At first, this was awkward and difficult and required a lot of failing forward on my part.

In hindsight, it was one of the best learning experiences in my career. I learned the characteristics of a FIT organization and teams and the role played by empathy and humility in leadership. I learned the importance of engagement, learning people's purpose and the importance of serving others. The concept of FIT was taking root in my mind and actions. I must have passed the test when Rob and the Ellis family eventually asked me to run their South Beloit business.

Group Stretch

The biggest job you have as a FIT leader is to direct and motivate the masses. Most leaders hate to admit just how much of a struggle this can be. They become boxed in by their own lack of creativity, or they simply don't know who's working for them. Crafting a sense of urgency around your FIT mission is vital to shaping success in your organization. It's the most productive way to get your people on board and in the right seats, or off the bus altogether if necessary.

Jim with Earl

Getting acquainted with people is an exciting perk of leadership, especially when you meet someone like Earl. He's a vibrant man in his midtwenties who works at Perdue's plant in Dothan, Alabama. Upon making my rounds on the production floor at Dothan, I heard sporadic cheers and shouts coming from his direction. Earl was ramping up laughter as he led the group of hourly associates in their ritual preshift stretching exercises. I was impressed with this display of engagement and enthusiasm. He understood people, and better yet, he liked them—the makings of a great leader.

I saw Earl later that day from the front of the training center during my address to the Dothan plant. I couldn't resist the opportunity to showcase what I'd seen, and I asked Earl to join me, assured he wouldn't mind the extra crowd time. He didn't disappoint with a company-wide group-stretch demonstration. The crowd was smiling, laughing, and fully engaged in the moment. Earl set the tone, and the meeting was a huge success.

Get to know your culture as if you were an outsider visiting the office. Create brown-bag lunch forums with guest panels featuring staff members to glean from otherwise hidden areas of expertise. Social psychology is as simple as a lunch date. Be a participant, sit in and learn something about what makes other people tick, and then you'll know exactly what's needed to get your people on board.

The worst thing a leader can do is to get too comfortable sitting in his high-backed office chair. Take a field trip outside the office and go talk to the interns. If you really want to impress them, memorize their names—not because you have to, but because you want to. People will rarely come to you; they don't always feel comfortable talking to a hands-folded suit behind a desk. Show up at the soda machine or get in on the production floor for a group stretch.

Being Creative

Imagination is something my dad used on obstacles in his path. As a cookie and cracker salesman for Archway, he was incorrigible in the best way. When A&P grocery stores refused to carry his product, he expected a good reason for it. The store manager insisted there was no shelf space for his product and politely said "No thank you," hoping he would go away. He did, long enough to construct a display that fit neatly on the end of A&P's aisleway. He returned to A&P with it proudly in tow. Robbed of their excuse, the store accepted his product.

My father's spirit of resolve and his love for people is something I carry with me to this day. It inspires me to examine my own position in life and consider whether I've allowed my own success to be shaped by another person's "no." That's when I reload my grit quotient, and power through.

I'm convinced that my dad preferred life as a challenge. "If someone insists there's no shelf space for you," he told me, "just bring your own."

When a local grocery chain that carried my father's products was faced with a strike, he personally drove a route truck to the back of one of the stores and delivered his product to the shelves to ensure the store was well-stocked. He was always creative in helping others win, even when it was inconvenient for him.

He believed it was unfair to ask someone to do what you wouldn't be willing to do yourself. I've added to this belief that it's unreasonable to ask team members to do something in their professional life that they're either unwilling or unable to do in their personal life. If a colleague can't balance her checking account, I don't want her to be my CFO. By putting others in an unFIT situation, you're not serving them well. Instead you're setting yourself and your team up for disaster.

Chapter Twelve
A Closing Word

Early in this journey we faced a huge problem: that of unFIT leadership, organizations, and mind-sets. But when FIT leadership sinks deep into your environment, there's meaning for every stakeholder. We all desire to play a part in something greater than ourselves, something that's an inbuilt, natural expression of our purpose.

We long to be part of the solution—and as doers, we are.

You've read this book because there's something you hope to do with your life, your team, your family, or your organization. There's a dream you envision in the not-too-distant future. Maybe you want to change careers, go back to school, or finally get that promotion. Maybe your team wants to build something of lasting value. Maybe your organization wants to put a dent in the universe by enhancing the quality of life for everyone they touch.

If you're still holding on to hope, it's time to act on it in real time and space. Seasons of life will come and go, demanding things from you—but if you're steadfast, you'll see this desired vision come to pass.

Running legend Steve Prefontaine, who spearheaded the 1970s running movement, has an oft-quoted saying: "To give anything less than your best is to sacrifice the gift." Discovering your purpose and creating a Fully Integrated Team is about empowering this gift through every conceivable means.

I couldn't think of a more natural way to end this discussion on life, leadership, and FIT than to say that once you've found your gift, never sacrifice it. Share your gift with others, using grit, compassion, and humility—and you'll be amazed at what you get back.

Life is not about money, or fame, or popular opinion, or any kind of trivial pursuit that steals your sense of meaning. The world is full of people who have already sacrificed this. But it's an optimist's game: Do what makes you come alive, and don't be surprised when others follow suit behind you.

This is the mark of a true leader...a leader of Fully Integrated Teams.

Notes

Chapter 3

1. Daniel Pink, *A Whole New Mind: Why Right-Brainers Will Rule the Future* (New York: Riverhead Books, 2005), 35.

2. Viktor Frankl, *Man's Search for Meaning* (Washington Square Press, 1984), 103–104.

Chapter 4

1. James C. Collins and Jerry I. Porras, "Building Your Company's Vision," *Harvard Business Review,* September/October 1996, reprint no. 96501, http://hbr.org/product/building-your-company-s-vision/an/96501-PDF-ENG.

2. Warren Bennis and Patricia Ward Biederman, *The Essential Bennis* (San Francisco: Jossey-Bass, 2009), 198–199.

Chapter 5

1. Sangeeth Varghese, "The Real Value of Happiness at Work," Forbes.com, June 28, 2010, www.forbes.com/2010/06/28/happiness-srikumar-rao-leadership-managing-varghese.html.

Chapter 6

1. Norman Doidge, *The Brain That Changes Itself* (New York: Penguin Books, 2007), 209.

2. Bruce Lipton, *The Biology of Belief: Unleashing the Power of Consciousness, Matter, & Miracles* (Hay House, 2008), 7.

Chapter 7

1. Theodore Roosevelt, "Man in the Arena" quote from "Citizenship in a Republic" speech at the Sorbonne, Paris, April 23, 1910, http://theodoreroosevelt.org/life/quotes.htm.

2. Mary Fischer, "California's Matrix One Is Where the Elite Meet to Beat Their Bodies into Concrete," People.com archive, January 30, 1984, http://www.people.com/people/archive/article/0,,20086963,00.html.

3. Diane Coutu, "How Resilience Works," *HBR's 10 Must Reads: On Managing Yourself* (Harvard Business School Publishing, 2009), PDF digital file.

Chapter 10

1. Simon Sinek, *Start with Why: How Great Leaders Inspire Everyone to Take Action* (New York: Portfolio, 2009), 158.

Chapter 11

1. Jim Collins and Morten T. Hansen, *Great by Choice: Uncertainty, Chaos, and Luck—Why Some Thrive Despite Them All* (New York: Harper-Collins, 2011), 1.